Out of the Doubles Kitchen

A Memoir of the First Family of Doubles
The Number One Street Food of Trinidad & Tobago

Badru Deen

Published by Caritrade, Inc. 7720 SW 168 Terrace, Miami, FL 33157, USA.
Email: outofthedoubleskitchen@gmail.com
Website: www.outofthedoubleskitchen.com

Foreword

"*Out of the Doubles Kitchen*" is an extraordinary narrative of "Doubles," the most popular street food of Trinidad and Tobago and the foundation for the rich history of the Deen family. What is even more remarkable is the fact that Badru Deen has had the foresight and determination to undertake this trailblazing work of establishing his family's innovation in indentureship cuisine and registering their contribution to the nation.

MamooDeen's creation of Doubles and his mastery as an exponent of Indian classical songs are testimonies of what the author calls "creativity out of poverty". Trinidad and Tobago's steelband, calypso, chutney music, Tassa drums and so much more demonstrate the fact, that poverty can indeed be a powerful incubator of creativity.

MamooDeen's experiment grew into a successful enterprise but the contribution of his wife, Rasulan, is equally inspiring. She was the "propelling rear wheel of Mamoo-Deen's freight bike in the Doubles business." Her life story gives the reader a powerful glimpse of the trials and tribulations of East Indian women, in the early Trinidad and Tobago's Plantation Society.

"*Out of the Doubles Kitchen*" not only establishes Doubles as the king of street foods in Trinidad and Tobago but also validates Badru Deen as a biographer whose story about the fascinating journey of East Indians from India to Trinidad and beyond, is bound to inspire readers across the globe. The author is correct in stating that the study of Doubles is a case study of self-sufficiency, hard work and persistence. The lives of most descendants of East Indian Immigrants who came to Trinidad and Tobago are testimonies of this fact.

This book will help to create a greater appreciation of the East Indians' contribution to the development of Trinidad and Tobago.

–H.E. Mr. Chandradath Singh
High Commissioner of Trinidad and Tobago to India, Japan, Indonesia, Sri Lanka, Singapore, and Bangladesh.

Delhi, India
October 28, 2013

Dedication

This memoir is dedicated to my parents, Emamool and Rasulan Deen, who taught me that "simplicity is the ultimate sophistication" and independence is gained from an entrepreneurial endeavor.

To my brothers, Jamaloo and Shamal, who assumed the family's Doubles business responsibilities and our father's dream, which I abandoned.

To my brother Edool who joined me in thinking outside the "Doubles Box."

To my sister Sharm who was a second mother to Edool, Shamal and me when we needed our mother the most.

To James West, who broke down the first barrier to my upward mobility in the Trinidad and Tobago Public Service Commission.

To my parents-in-law, James and Baby Ramsingh, who recognized my human potential, paid my airfare to Canada to attend university, and facilitated the owning of our first home.

To Leslie Kumar Misir, my teacher in Gandhi Memorial Vedic Elementary School, for beseeching my mother to send me to high school.

To Jose (Pepe) de la Torriente, for choosing me to join his corporate team in Miami.

To my wife, Grace, who sacrificed her ambitions for mine and our children's.

To my grandson Ameet, whose Down's Syndrome condition is teaching me that all my so-called life's struggles were truly insignificant when compared with the challenges of a differently-abled human being.

TRINIDAD AND TOBAGO

Charlotteville
Castara
Moriah   Roxborough
Plymouth   Belle
                 Garden
Mount   Scarborough
Pleasant

TOBAGO

C a r i b e a n

S e a

Toco
Galera Pt.
Blanchisseuse
Las Cuevas   Matelot
                    Redhead
Maraval   Maracas   Cumaca
                              ATLANTIC
           Tunapuna   *OCEAN*
VENEZUELA   Salibea
     Dragons Port of   Arima
     Mouth   Spain   San
              Juan
         Tunapuna   Sangre
                Cumuto Grande
    Chaguanas
                 El Quemado   *TRINIDAD*
    Carapichaima
    California Tabaquite   Biche
Gulf
of   Rio Claro   Guatuaro Pt.
Paria San Fernando Princes   Saint Joseph
                       Town   Tableland Pierreville
    Brighton   Débé   Cipero
    Point Fortin   Sainte Croix
                                    Guayaguayare
         Siparia Peñal   Basse
Fullarton   Terre   Galeota Pt.
                    Moruga
Serpents   San Francique
Mouth

Contents

Chapter 1:
Why a Book about Doubles

Doubles, the number one street food in Trinidad, was created in 1936, in Princes Town, Trinidad and Tobago, in the West Indies, by my parents, Emamool Deen, a.k.a. MamooDeen (January 24, 1917–March 13, 1979), and Raheman Rasulan Deen (April 20, 1920–November 1, 1994).

By relating the authentic oral history of Doubles, this memoir sets out to correct a historical oversight in which the truth of the origin of Doubles needed to be rescued from the edge of oblivion. It provides a better understanding of my parents' involvement in a famous historical event that became a national heritage. It describes my early years growing up in the first family of Doubles and its influence on my experiments with upward social mobility. It also invokes posterity as my motivation to write it. I do not have a monopoly on my history but instead share it with my parents' posterity. This memoir will preserve the knowledge of the origin of Doubles and fulfill my desire to pass on the family's Doubles legacy to future generations.

The Deens' genealogy became distorted under colonialism and illiteracy. Our ancestral origin is believed to be somewhere in Uttar Pradesh, India, but the precise location remains unknown. Since our ancestral surname is not Deen, our functional ancestry therefore begins in Trinidad with Emamool Deen and Rasulan Ali in 1917 and 1920, respectively. (A link to the family tree may be accessed on the website: www.outofthedoubleskitchen.com)

My mother was a great storyteller who possessed the remarkable ability to digress on a digression and return to the original story without missing a beat, and still keep us riveted to the storyline. Her storytelling skills were honed to teach, entertain, and enthrall us, her nine children, who did not have the luxury of books, radio, television, or video games to pique our curiosity and imagination. She was our true multimedia mom. Had she been literate, the story of Doubles would most certainly have been written by her. So, in her honor I assume that responsibility.

The need to record the history of Doubles crystallized in my mind when others began to usurp the credit for creating Doubles. People who know the history started calling me and my siblings, pleading with us to correct this factual inaccuracy. Since only the oral history of Doubles exists in Trinidad and it was already becoming blurred by misinformation, as a son of the creator of Doubles, I felt obligated to fill the information void and validate the oral history by documenting and videotaping the testimonials of eyewitnesses. Thus, I became an intentional writer and started this memoir on June 1, 2010. As the executor of my father's estate, I had access to birth certificates, documents, old family photos, and audiovisual recordings, which proved invaluable for this writing exercise. Coming from a home with no books to actually writing one is a quantum leap of faith in my desire, as one of the custodians of these memories, to communicate my family's history through the written word and leave an informational gift to my parents' posterity and social historians, especially in Trinidad and Tobago and its diaspora.

A Street Food Called Doubles

Doubles is an Indo-Trinidadian vegan delicacy made of spicy curried *chana* (chickpeas) served with a choice of chutneys between two *baras* (fried breads made from seasoned, enriched, all-purpose flour). The sandwich is wrapped and served in paper. Before the advent of greaseproof paper, the original Doubles were served in plain brown Hercules paper.

It is plausibly assumed that Doubles evolved from the Indian dish *chole bhature* (also called *chana bhatura*), which is a combination of chole (*chana masala*), spicy chickpeas, and *bhature* (*poori*)—a fried puffy bread made of *maida* flour, which is used in the making of Indian pastries and breads.

Chole bhature is served with onions and *achar* (Indian pickle) and commonly eaten in northern India. It is served with one bhature, from which pieces are broken off to scoop up, or *bore,* the chole and is not presented as a self-contained chickpea sandwich like Doubles. Having eaten chole bhature in Delhi, Haridwar, Rishikesh, and Varanasi, I can attest to the taste and culinary differences between chole bhature and Doubles. They are literally worlds apart, as Trinidadian curries and chutneys have evolved with their own creatively distinctive presentation, ingredients, and taste characteristics.

The Popularity of Doubles

On almost every busy street corner in Trinidad, you can find a Doubles vendor surrounded by salivating customers awaiting their turn to savor this culinary delight. Above the din of the vehicular and pedestrian traffic, you can hear the Doubles patrons placing their orders using a vocabulary unique to this street food. They holler phrases such as, "Gimme ah Doubles with plenty pepper" or "ah Doubles with slight (pepper)" or "ah Doubles with no pepper." What started as an early morning breakfast treat is now available throughout the day and into the late night. Doubles "hit the spot" for Trinidadians on the go.

This street food, Doubles, enjoys remarkable recognition. In-transit international pilots and flight attendants make a beeline for the Doubles vendors at Piarco International Airport to take Doubles back on their return flights. Doubles were featured on the US Travel Channel show *Bizarre Foods with Andrew Zimmern,* during which he showcased his enjoyment of the delicacy that certainly was not "bizarre."

During the longest parliamentary debate in the history of Trinidad and Tobago on March 2–3, 2012, which lasted about twenty-seven hours, the House of Representatives recessed for Doubles.

On August 10, 2012, Lalone Gordon, double bronze-medal winner for Trinidad and Tobago in the London 2012 Olympics, stated that after spending more than a fortnight in cool and sometimes cold London, he was looking forward to some warmth. "We coming home for Doubles," he declared. A double Olympic-medal winner craves Doubles, the best

Trini comfort food for champions! Doubles have captured the nation's palette like no other street food.

The Doubles phenomenon has followed the Trinidadian diaspora to the ethnic enclaves of major cities like Fort Lauderdale, London, Miami, New York, Toronto, and Winnipeg. In their new homes away from home, the Trinidadian diaspora nostalgically savors this delicacy, which virtually transports them back to their homeland, even if only momentarily.

Chapter 2: Descendants of Indentured Laborers

I was born on September 5, 1945, a hundred years after my ancestors first arrived in Trinidad from India. After the emancipation of the African slaves in 1838, the British colonists imported indentured laborers from India to fill the labor void created by the emancipated slaves in the sugar and cocoa industries. The contrived labor scheme lasted seventy-two years, from 1845 to 1917.

My birth was a home delivery in Fairfield, Princes Town, on the island of Trinidad. My native country is made up of Trinidad and Tobago, the most southerly of the chain of Caribbean islands. The population of 1.2 million is made up of East Indians, 40 percent; Africans, 37.5 percent; mixed, 20.5 percent; and others, 2 percent (2000 census).

Seventh of Nine Children

My mother said I was born on a bright, moonlit night with my amniotic sac intact and that I actually hit the floor before the arrival of Ms. Kate, the village midwife. The prevailing superstition was that a baby born with his or her amniotic sac intact would become a clairvoyant; I am still awaiting the outcome of this omen to perceive things beyond the natural range of the senses. I was the seventh of nine children and the fourth of six boys.

I was a sickly baby who cried incessantly. The crying continued into early childhood and did not stop even after my father dipped me headfirst into a barrel of water and then placed me in some bushes nearby to scare the crying out of me. Nothing worked. They said I sometimes continued the crying episodes nonstop for a half day. With this behavior, I earned the nickname "Half-Day" from some of my close relatives.

I remember crying late at nights, when Ma would heat some tea over the flame of a pitch-oil lamp and the tea would taste like the smoke from the lamp. Since I did not have any major diseases or illnesses, I think I cried for the attention of my mother, who was too busy in the Doubles business and taking care of the other six children at the same time.

Two years later my younger brother Shamal was born, on September 26, 1947. This made me cry even more because I was now also competing for my mother's attention with a new baby. On August 5, 1950, Edool, the last child, was born, bringing to an end, at age thirty, my mother's thirteen continuous years of childbearing that produced nine children. Edool would continue to breast-feed until he was five years old. No wonder I cried so much!

All of us nine children called our father Papa, and all but the twins called our mother Ma or *Moy*—a form of *Mai*, Hindi for mother. The twins, who were the firstborn children and who spoke Hindi fluently with our parents, called our mother *Daye*—a shortened form of *Didaye*, from *Didi*, Hindi for sister—because that was how they heard her younger siblings address her.

My teenage twin brothers and older siblings assisted our parents in caring for and raising me and the younger ones. They filled the void created by a busy mother who constantly worked in the Doubles Kitchen and a hardworking but truant father who strayed after his vices and who, even when he was at home, was undemonstrative about his love for his family. The younger siblings called the twins *Big Bhaiya* and *Lil Bhaiya*, "Hinglish" for "big brother" and "small brother." The Hindi word *bhaiya* also carries a measure of respect for the older siblings.

There was no hugging and kissing in my family. I never heard my parents say to themselves or to me the words "I love you." They never touched each other in our presence or in public. We had to recognize love in their actions, not words. We grew up not realizing that we needed to be loved demonstrably, because we did not feel deprived of love. We sensed the presence of love in the family.

My parents never addressed each other by name. It was a cultural custom for showing respect for each other. The nearest they came to saying each other's names was with the use of the pronoun "you," as in, "You heard what I said?" or "Are you there?" I inherited some of these family traits from my early childhood and had to learn to say "I love you" to my own two children, and when I did, it used to feel a little awkward.

My Father: MamooDeen

Although my father's nickname, MamooDeen, means Uncle Deen in Hindi, it was really a shortened version of Emamool

Deen. His name on his birth certificate reads Emamooldeen, with no last name mentioned. It was the best spelling that the recorder of births could have interpreted for the Arabic name Imam ul-Dīn, which means "leader of the righteous way." My father was called Deen for short, which evolved into his surname and which he passed on to his nine children.

Born January 22, 1917, in Poona, Piparo, Trinidad, he was the oldest of five children of his mother, Hasmath Baksh, and his father, Imam "Bombay" Baksh. His siblings were one brother, Babwa, and three sisters, Kasidan, Rosidan, and Nabidan. His mother died in childbirth when Nabidan was born.

The absence of a mother threw young MamooDeen into a parental role, cooking and taking care of his younger siblings while his father worked as an itinerant barber. In raising his siblings, he developed a paternalistic nature that would remain the hallmark of the man throughout his life.

Shortly after the death of his mother, their house was accidentally burned by his eleven-year-old brother Babwa, who was trying to light the firewood in the *chulha* (a woodburning stove handmade from mud and clay). He used a lighted flambeau, made from a glass bottle containing pitch oil and a piece of cloth rag inserted as a wick, to light a piece of the edge of the thatch *carat* roof, thinking that once it was lit, he would break off the lighted piece and transfer it to the chulha, but his puerile judgment cost the family their house. When his father returned from work that day, MamooDeen and his sisters have related, Babwa received a flogging that almost killed the young boy. The property was thereafter repossessed by MamooDeen's maternal relatives, leaving the family homeless and landless.

Bombay knew a lady who operated a restaurant in Princes Town. Restaurants were called "cook shops." The restaurant owner was a single mother with three daughters and a son. She took the homeless family in and later married Bombay. MamooDeen's baby sister, Nabidan, was adopted by relatives in Avocat in the southern part of the island. By helping out in the lady's restaurant, young MamooDeen honed his cooking skills, which would influence the rest of his life and the lives of many.

In his early teens, MamooDeen started to work for the British plantation owners at the Craignish sugar estate. Because of his personality and good looks, he said, they employed him as a "yard boy" to be at their beck and call for the fixed income of one shilling (twenty-four cents) per day. With this income, he bought his first bicycle, a Raleigh, the top brand-name bicycle, which mobilized his life.

My Mother: Rasulan

Less than two miles east of Princes Town was the agrarian village of Fairfield, a predominantly patriarchal Indian community that lived by specific value systems and norms that were based primarily on oral traditions.

In this village lived a family of nine children: five boys and four girls. Their father, Samtali Nanhoo Ali, became a widower when his wife, Majidan, died in childbirth with Cassim. Rasulan was the fourth child of the family, a girl born April 26, 1920. Her name, from the Arabic Rasula, means "messenger." Sahidan ("Syde") was the firstborn, followed by two brothers, Asgar and Ashraf "Choate "Ali. The nickname Choate is derived from *chota bhai,* Hindi for "younger brother."

After her mother's death, Rasulan, at about ten years old, became the "mother" of the house, especially to her five younger siblings: Yatali, Tinia, Ding Ding, Babe, and baby Cassim. With these imposed maternal responsibilities in an oral culture, formal education, especially for an Indian village girl, was the least important survival tool for a family of nine, who needed all hands to grow what they ate. They built their own house and lived without regularly making purchases in the marketplace. The family relied on subsistence farming for their survival. They planted small quantities of sugarcane, rice, vegetables, and ground provisions, and tended to a few cattle, goats, and chickens, which most families in the village owned out of necessity and for self-sufficiency. The cultivation of sugarcane generated a minimum income during the annual harvest time.

Cassim was mentally challenged. Living in his own contemplative world, he spoke few words. Even in his adulthood he needed supervision. In the family's struggle for survival, his needs seemed neglected. Speech therapy was nonexistent in the village, and the family resigned themselves to accepting his condition as God's intention. He grew up to be a gentle giant who contributed to the family's welfare with his brute strength. He lifted heavy bales of grass for the animals and performed other chores requiring manpower, such as lifting heavy bundles of cut sugarcane onto bull carts. The family believed that the cause of his condition was his difficult birth, in which his mother died giving him life.

An Arranged Marriage

The similarities of my parents' early life experiences were striking—both being burdened at a tender age with raising their younger siblings. With overwhelming domestic responsibilities, education was not an option for them. The system did not have a safety net like the welfare system in modern societies. However, this was a blessing in disguise: it required their survival instincts to rely on their basic human creative abilities. For the ambitious, creativity is a function of poverty—the poorer you are, the more creative you must become.

The colonial plantation system was designed to perpetuate the poverty of the workers. David Korten wrote in *The Great Turning* that "poverty is an inevitable product of an unjust system designed to exploit those who work hard and play by the rules."

At nineteen, MamooDeen became friends with Rasulan's brothers, Asgar and Choate. He would ride his bicycle from Princes Town to visit them frequently in Fairfield. They would play cricket or just hang out together (called "liming") in Fairfield's verdant, undulating countryside. The name Fairfield was so appropriate for this piece of beautiful and unpolluted countryside where man and nature interacted like an extended family supporting one another. The equal-opportunity fertile land produced crops abundantly, regardless of whether it was cultivated by exploited slaves and indentured laborers or by free men. When the sugarcane fields were in blossom, the cane arrow (tassels) made the landscape look like displaced blankets of snow under the tropical sun.

It was during these visits to this unspoiled countryside that MamooDeen set eyes on innocent Rasulan, noticing how she took care of the household and her younger siblings. As a caregiver to his own younger siblings, he recognized the maternal qualities Rasulan displayed in performing her domestic duties.

He told Asgar and Choate that Rasulan, with her demonstrated domestic abilities, would make him a good wife. He promised to have his father speak to their father about arranging a marriage between them.

Rasulan could never, in her deepest fantasy, imagine that this handsome, "fair-skinned town boy" would ever have eyes for her, a young, innocent peasant girl who considered herself unattractive due to her dark complexion, soiled clothing, and always being barefoot in the kitchen. By then she would have had two of the three qualifications of a typical village Indian housewife: barefoot, pregnant, and in the kitchen.

Her father Nanhoo's house, like the houses of other villagers, was made of a type of rattan material called *roseau* for the walls, with a thatch roof and dirt floor. The round roseau sticks were intricately tied together with vines to provide stability, privacy, and some protection from the elements and wild creatures. These sticks were plastered with mud, creating a smooth surface that would be *lipayed*—given a final coat of a mixture of liquid mud and cow dung with a rag, using bare hands.

The stove in the kitchen was the ubiquitous wood-burning chulha, hand-molded from clay/mud to hold the pots. Spaces near the pots were left for the wood fire to breathe and the flames to embrace the pots. The large opening in the front was for the firewood.

A wood-burning chulha

Nanhoo and Bombay met and immediately saw the opportunity to arrange not only for the marriage of Rasulan and MamooDeen but also for Choate and Asgar to marry Mamoo-Deen's two sisters, Rosidan and Kasidan. In short, Mamoo-Deen's two sisters would marry Rasulan's two brothers.

On June 6, 1936, a double wedding took place, with MamooDeen marrying Rasulan and Choate marrying Rosidan. Asgar and Kasidan were married at a later date. The double-wedding procession carried the two couples on bullock-drawn carts. They were married under Muslim rites. No rings were exchanged during their wedding ceremonies, mainly because custom did not demand it and their economic situation made such luxuries unattainable. Like Hindu marriages, Muslim marriages were not recognized in the British colony of Trinidad and Tobago at that time. As a result, the offspring of these unions were classified as illegitimate children. So the prevailing British laws in the early 1900s in Trinidad made the author a bastard!

As the extended family tradition dictated, Asgar and Choate took their wives to their father's house on Fairfield Road, and MamooDeen took his new bride to his father's rented wooden barracks on Bonanza Street in Princes Town. Bombay and his four children had moved there after he separated from the cook shop lady and became the imam of the nearby mosque. One of Rasulan's first duties was to light the mosque's pitch-oil lamp daily at sundown.

A family's unit in the barracks measured a hundred square feet of living space. These ubiquitous wooden barracks were originally built on the sugar estates to house African slaves, until their emancipation in 1838, and were later occupied by Indian laborers during their indentureship. They had no kitchen or bathroom, and the units were separated on the inside with wooden partitions that did not reach the roof, allowing ventilation in the tropical heat but no privacy. Cooking was done in an open-air fireside made of three large stones arranged to hold the pot. Wood was their only cooking fuel. Water was collected from rainfall or a nearby pond.

As was the custom, Rasulan returned to her father's home after three days of living at her in-laws' house. Maybe this was an unwritten escape clause for the bride if she strongly opposed the arranged marriage. While visiting her father's home, Rasulan was reunited with her three youngest siblings: Ding Ding, age seven; Babe, six; and Cassim, five. For these siblings, her absence for the three days was like déjà vu of losing their real mother, and their separation anxiety increased at the thought of her leaving again. Her maternal instincts and responsibilities kicked in, and she insisted on bringing them with her to her new hundred-square-foot barracks room that she was already sharing with her father-in-law and brother-in-law Babwa.

A dowry of a pair of chickens and a female goat, which Nanhoo presented to Rasulan, and MamooDeen's Raleigh bicycle were the material assets with which the newlyweds started their marital journey in Princes Town.

Princes Town

The Spanish reign over Trinidad lasted about three hundred years, from 1498 to 1802. Early in that period, the Spanish created settlements, similar to Native American and Canadian reservations, for the native Amerindians. They called these settlements "missions," where they proselytized the natives into Catholicism, taught them Spanish, and exploited their free labor. One of those missions was Mission Savana Grande, which was renamed Princes Town on January 20, 1880, by the British during their 160-year rule of the island. Princes Town, which the locals pronounce "Princess Town," was so named to commemorate the visit to the town of Queen Victoria's grandsons, Princes Edward Albert and George of Wales, who became King George V. The princes planted two of the local resplendent yellow *poui* trees (*Tabebuia)* on the grounds of Saint Stephen's Anglican Church, which still blossom in springtime.

Princes Town was destined to become a busy hub of commercial and administrative activities because of its strategic location connecting the towns of Barackpore, Moruga, Rio Claro, and Mayaro in the southeast; Debe and Siparia in the southwest; and the city of San Fernando to the west.

In addition to being the birthplace of Doubles, Princes Town has made some other significant contributions to the national identity. It is the birthplace of Yolande Pompey (1929–1979), a world-renowned light-heavyweight boxer who fought in fifty-five boxing matches and won thirty-eight (twenty-six in knockouts), lost twelve (KO five), and drew in five. In total he boxed 380 rounds with a KO percentage of 47.27. Princes Town is also the birthplace of Serjad Makmadeen, a.k.a. Joseph Charles, owner of Joseph Charles Bottling Works, producers of Solo Beverages. The red Solo soft drink especially became the preferred complement to spicy Doubles.

The town's most important contribution to the nation, however, was not a street food, a soft drink or a boxer, but a political fighter: Mr. Basdeo Panday, who was born in Saint Julien Village, Princes Town, in 1933. He became the first Indo-Trinidadian prime minister of the nation in 1995. From the arrival of the first Indian indentured laborers in 1845, it took 150 years for them to arrive in the corridors of political power to govern the nation. So Princes Town contributed to breaking down not only the barriers to Indian cuisine but also the political barriers to Indian leadership and governance.

The Influence of Indentureship

With his new responsibilities of supporting a wife and an extended family, MamooDeen knew that laboring as a general servant for the Englishman at Craignish sugar estate, which included bathing "hog cattle" (water buffaloes), for one shilling per day would not suffice. He quit the Craignish sugar estate and found employment loading and transporting sugarcane from the fields to the factory, driving a mule-drawn cart for "long days and short pay," he would say. He was still not satisfied with this new job, which was more physically demanding and paid only a little more than his previous job. He believed he was worth more and wished for a more lucrative and satisfying employment.

Poverty and the culture of subservience in which my parents' early experiences were steeped were the direct result of the British indenture system that created an institutional and pervasive condition of exclusion. This new version of slavery that the British concocted, exploited the cheap labor of Indians and their descendants even after the indentureship ended.

When MamooDeen was born in 1917, the indignities of subhuman existence that his indentured grandparents endured were still inescapable. The prevailing political and economic systems supported the privilege and extravagance of the colonial masters and their corporate agents, not the workers. Although indentured laborers worked for a fixed, nonnegotiable wage of one shilling per day for the duration of their indenture and were promised a return passage to India at the end of the contracted period, they were entrapped by the same laws and infrastructure that were established for the African slaves. Every aspect of their lives was controlled, even their freedom of movement from place to place, which required "passes." The British had promised the workers freedom from their miserable lives in India but instead provided them with conditions of slavery. These human cargoes were a sanctioned version of human trafficking.

To paraphrase Thomas Jefferson, slavery and the British indenture system waged a cruel war against human nature itself, violating its most sacred rights of life and liberty in the persons of a distant people who offended no one but were brought into servitude in another hemisphere.

Illiteracy

The well-dressed, handsome, fair-skinned, strong, and affable young specimen of a man that was MamooDeen was very popular. His popularity boosted his self-esteem and confidence. He felt he could succeed in anything he tried and equated his charismatic charm to his salesmanship. However, when he tried to convince a shopkeeper to hire him for counter sales, he was unsuccessful. He was unable to read the word *evaporated* and said it was milk when asked to describe the product. The shopkeeper found him unqualified and did not offer him the position.

This illiterate grandson of Indian indentured laborers, with an equally illiterate wife, trapped in poverty, staring at the faces of their hungry extended family, relied on their independent energetic spirit to overcome necessity. Giving up was not an option; instead, they gave all to survive those unforgiving circumstances.

The agrarian lifestyle always beckoned to MamooDeen's reserve of physical energy, but he wanted something different—a job that would be more lucrative than the pittance earned for exploiting his physical strength. He sensed that the job he was fantasizing about did not exist, so he would have to create it. His frustration with the cycle of poverty would have to find expression in his creativity.

He always defended his illiteracy confidently by saying, "Sense was made before book," and, "Common sense is better than book sense." He was proud of his common sense, which he would remind us was not very common. His life's circumstances motivated him to challenge the compelling evidence that literacy is an indispensable means for effective social and economic participation and advancement in life, thus contributing to human development and poverty reduction.

MamooDeen's life's mission was to prove he could survive without formal education. He believed that despite his illiteracy, he was still free to create and come up with innovative ideas; he sensed that education was not in college degrees and certificates but in the person, and so he looked for solutions from within. His creativity had a primordial characteristic that did not rely on literacy to manifest itself. In learning how to survive in his environment, he had to concentrate on his skills to overcome his immediate challenges, rather than focus on the luxury of an education that did not define his talent and intelligence. Paper qualifications were not necessary for him to learn and improve the quality of his impoverished life. He set out to prove that the common man has the capacity and resourcefulness, derived from the wisdom of the villages, to succeed despite his circumstances. Illiteracy was not a barrier to his learning, developing, and contributing, because he understood that the lack of education was not a measure of his intelligence.

He also associated education with the colonial masters who callously exploited illiterate slaves and indentured laborers for economic gain. He was very distrustful of "educated people," primarily because he saw education as a colonial tool used to instill conformity and obedience, neither of which he adhered to. In this respect, MamooDeen was indeed, proudly, a "recalcitrant Indian." Spending his time on creative problem solving and learning life skills was his main focus. He assimilated a few ideas and made them his life and character, which Vivekananda describes as "having more education than any man who has learned by heart a whole library."

To MamooDeen, imagination and resourcefulness were more important than memorization of knowledge contained in books. In his world, sitting and reading a book was not real work because it did not involve physical labor. To sit and read was to be a *jangar chor*—literally a thief of other people's labor or strength, or a lazy person depending on the efforts of others. I was called a "jangar chor" many times when caught reading a book instead of helping out in the family business. When the firstborn twins were found reading comic books, MamooDeen became suspicious of their contents. He confiscated and burned the comic books in the firesides of the Doubles Kitchen. My father saw reading as a passive activity of studying someone else's history, which he deemed an idle pursuit. He believed that to work physically was to create actively one's own history. Like Henry Ford, he believed in "showing him what you have done instead of telling him what you know."

The normal survival mode of village life that relied on physical strength certainly justified this way of thinking. The repercussions of this early conditioning still make me apprehensive whenever I read a book—and even as I write this one, I feel I should be doing something more physically productive, like taking out the garbage.

Illiteracy did not deter my parents' ambition to succeed as a husband and wife entrepreneurial team. What mattered was that they had an idea for a potential business that could solve their economic predicament. MamooDeen had the ability to overcome setbacks that would have sent other young village men back to the cane fields. He knew how to find opportunities where none seemed to exist. He had the ability to re-create.

Necessity became their catalyst for invention and creativity. From their prison of poverty, MamooDeen and Rasulan creatively decided to use their cooking skills, in which they were both competent from being caregivers to their younger siblings, to alleviate their economic hardship. In being themselves, they knew they had to fit in where they belonged.

The British, to accomplish their capitalistic objectives, had adopted a system of labor exploitation that first used slaves, then indentured laborers, and, finally, wage slaves. MamooDeen refused to be a wage slave. He refused to remain in servility and suffer in silence. With pride, he turned his back on the system, not wanting to be a pawn in the power games of the colonial masters operating through their corporate agents in the sugar estates. He had the determination and commitment to change his paradigm from a wage slave to an entrepreneur.

These two subsistence peasants, MamooDeen and Rasulan, radically and innovatively escaped their social circumstances in a leap of faith and became entrepreneurs in a nonagrarian activity. It was, in a sense, an act of resistance against the economic system of labor exploitation, subservience, and poor living conditions.

Chapter 3: The Origin of Doubles

Chickpeas

The chickpea (*Cicer arietinum*), also called chana, garbanzo bean, Indian pea, cece bean, and Bengal gram, is the third most important pulse crop of the world. It was originally cultivated around 3000 BC on the lands bordering Iraq and the Eastern Mediterranean. The area extends west to North, North East, and East Africa; north to Slovakia, Ukraine; and east to West China. From the Middle East, chickpeas spread to India. They are now also grown in many warm-temperate and subtropical regions. Today, the top ten producers are India, Pakistan, Turkey, Australia, Iran, Myanmar, Canada, Ethiopia, Mexico, and Iraq, in that order.

Chickpeas were grown by ancient Egyptians, Greeks, and Romans and were very popular among these cultures. In ancient Rome, the chickpea was so highly valued that one leader, Cicero, was proud to claim that his family name came from the Latin term for it, *Cicer arietinum*.

The oldest variety of chickpea is the desi type. It is small, angular, and variegated in color. Scholars believe desi chickpeas originated in Turkey and were subsequently introduced to India, where the most common form of chickpea is the kabuli, which is beige-colored with a larger beaked seed and a smoother coat. The name is derived from Kabul, Afghanistan, from where it was introduced to India in the eighteenth century.

It was the kabuli type, among other staples of grains, spices, and pulses, that was brought to Trinidad on the ships that transported indentured laborers from India between 1845 and 1917. The three-month journeys required a stock of familiar foods from the laborers' homeland. International trading companies subsequently supplied Trinidad with kabuli from the Middle East as well. Canada in recent years has been supplying Trinidad with kabuli. It is this kabuli type of chickpea that is used in the making of Doubles.

The nutritional value of chickpeas, or chana—the main ingredient of Doubles—is described by the United States Department of Agriculture (USDA) as follows:

> Chickpeas are a helpful source of zinc, folate and protein. They are also very high in dietary fiber and hence a healthy source of carbohydrates for persons with insulin sensitivity or diabetes. Chickpeas are low in fat and most of this is polyunsaturated. One hundred grams of mature boiled chickpeas contains 164 calories, 2.6 grams of fat (of which only 0.27 grams is saturated), 7.6 grams of dietary fiber and 8.9 grams of protein. Chickpeas also provide dietary phosphorus (49–53 mg/100 g), with some sources citing the garbanzo's content as about the same as yogurt and

close to milk. Recent studies by government agencies have also shown that chickpeas can assist in lowering of cholesterol in the bloodstream.

MamooDeen convinced Rasulan to sell her goat for seven shillings and invested the proceeds in a few pounds of chana, cooking oil, salt, brown paper, and a hand basket. The ingredients and packaging materials that started their first business venture were bought from Rahamut's Store in Princes Town and Masala Sadhu's in Craignish.

My parents soaked the chickpeas overnight, then fried them early the next day. They added onions, garlic, salt, and hot peppers, and then wrapped small quantities in cone-shaped brown-paper packs through which the oil would permeate. They filled the hand basket with about two hundred of these cone packs, and MamooDeen headed to the town center on foot, offering his snack packs to the public at one cent per pack. The town center of Princes Town and the cinema patrons during show times became his first target market.

Hindi was commonly spoken among the village Indians, and when English, their second language, was attempted, the resulting dialect became "Hinglish," so MamooDeen's first street cry for his crispy fried chickpeas was *"kripsy chana-dry chana."*

With an empty basket and a pocket full of coins, he returned home to Rasulan, who was anxiously awaiting the result of his first day's sales. When he emptied his pocket of the coins, Rasulan's anxiety turned to satisfaction for a job well done. MamooDeen's sales target was any amount that would exceed the twenty-four cents he was paid at the sugar estate. After covering his expenses, he easily exceeded that sum. He was convinced that his idea had merit and saw in a grain of chana the seed of his destiny. He envisioned his future in chana and was proud to be called by his trade name: "Chanaman." He created his own title and identity; he was no longer one of the "sheeple" of the plantation culture.

MamooDeen was confident that he could sell enough fried chana to recover his initial investment of seven shillings and generate an income that would exceed the pittance he earned at the Craignish sugar estate. He was determined to be his own boss and never work for anyone again. He and Rasulan were hardworking cooks with a vision. They were going to cook their way out of poverty. It was a critical turning point when they sensed the distinction between living on the return on capital and living on the return from selling their manual labor and decided to become an independent owner versus a dependent worker.

The Genesis of Doubles

Shortly afterward, they diversified the product line by introducing spicy boiled-and-fried chana, which they called *goognee* and which they also sold in the funnel-shaped packs. They then introduced boiled curried chana, which was sold from an enamel bowl in the basket, spooned out on brown Hercules paper cut to size. This was the genesis of Doubles. MamooDeen's "wet and dry chana" became his updated street cry. The encouraging sales motivated him to experiment further with the curried chana.

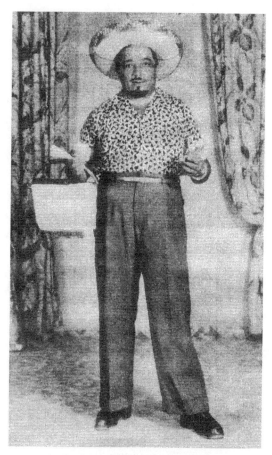

**MamooDeen with hand basket holding
cone-shaped packs of fried chana**

Before the creation of Doubles, *bara* was a known Indo
culinary delight. It was made with flour, turmeric, salt, and
ground mung beans called *urdi* in Hindi, and deep-fried
in coconut oil. The ground urdi would provide the protein;

the flour, the carbs; and the chutneys, made from mangoes, tamarind, and pommecythere (the local name for *Spondias dulcis,* or ambarella or golden apple), would make it a nutritiously delicious snack. One bara with the chutney of the day was sold as a single unit, usually at Indian festivals such as Ram Leela and Hosay and on government and estate paydays.

In a eureka moment, MamooDeen decided to incorporate his curried chana on a similar single bara with chutneys. It was an instant hit with his customers, and in no time they started to ask him to "double" the bara, making it more like a sandwich. This was the origin of the name Doubles, a plural word that describes the chana-and-bara sandwich. The humble slave barracks on Bonanza Street, Princes Town, became the incubator for the Doubles enterprise. In his entrepreneurial pursuit, the unlettered "Hinglish-speaking" MamooDeen contributed the word Doubles to the national lexicon.

For a little while longer, he continued selling the curried chana on a single bara, but Doubles soon became the product of choice for his customers, and Deen's Doubles became the pioneering brand of Doubles. The name MamooDeen became synonymous with Doubles in Princes Town.

Rasulan knew her destiny would be in the kitchen and, like the caged bird that sings, she resigned herself to that fate. She acquiesced in seeing herself as a passive player in their story. She was unassertive about her identity and became the supportive spouse behind the aspiring entrepreneur. She was like the propelling rear wheel of MamooDeen's freight bike in the Doubles business. She collaborated with him to create, from their makeshift kitchen, a new enterprise that they never could have imagined would have the possibility to change the nation's palette and grow to become the number one national street food of Trinidad and Tobago.

To MamooDeen and Rasulan, Doubles represented their triumph over the harsh agrarian system. From a prison of domination and poverty, they chose to live a different story that created a better personal and national history. They dug deep under the surface of their shame, pessimism, and fear of change with the only tools available to them: their self-confidence and a vision of their human possibility. They liberated themselves and transformed their lives from the trance induced by an oppressive system that had reduced uneducated laborers to a state of resigned dependence. They had sufficient knowledge to solve their problems and to give wings to their creative energies.

MamooDeen and Rasulan created a food product that would not only support them financially but provide sustaining meals to their family members, who were their first "customers" to taste-test the daily production.

As the business progressed, the bara recipe would exclude the ground urdi because the protein of the chana in Doubles made the urdi nutritionally redundant. Eliminating urdi also helped minimize the cost of production.

From "Poor-People Food" to Multimillion-Dollar Industry

From this humble origin began an arduous journey endured by the first family of Doubles to market their new food product in an environment where consumers did not take it seriously. Indian curry dishes were mainly confined to the sugarcane-estate environment, where they were consumed by indentured Indians for survival, not fine dining. The introduction of Doubles by a grandson of indentured laborers to a plural population, where Indians were relegated to the lowest rungs of society, invited the ridicule of it being "poor-people food," and it had to endure as well the stigma associated with street foods. As a result, the early clientele to whom the product appealed were mainly poor, hungry schoolchildren; vagrants; and drunkards.

But what was created by a poor husband-and-wife team in their makeshift, open-air kitchen on wood-burning firesides made with stones, as a survival experiment catering to other poor folks, is today the street food of choice for the Trinidadian population on the go. An idea that started with an initial investment of seven shillings is now a multimillion-dollar industry that is providing lucrative self-employment to hundreds of hardworking people. For every Doubles vendor on the street, there are several people—usually family members—behind the scenes in the production of this street food. There are also companies and personnel involved with the importation, sales, and distribution of the imported and locally sourced ingredients and supplies for the Doubles business.

Most of the ingredients and supplies—chickpeas, vegetable oils, flour (refined locally), wrapping paper, and bags—that go into the production of Doubles are imported. Curries, salt, and other spices are blended locally from imported raw ingredients. The local input consists of such ingredients as mangoes, pommecytheres, tamarind, hot peppers, coconuts, and *bandhania* or *chadon beni* for making a variety of chutneys.

Nowadays, most people who have committed to the hard-work routine required to earn a living from the lucrative Doubles business are unaware of its humble origins and the peasant pioneers who created it. On one of my trips to Trinidad, my friend Najib and I stopped in Chaguanas for Doubles. In a conversation with the Doubles vendor, I asked her if she knew who created Doubles, and she responded no. I said, "What if I told you it was my father?" Her retort was, "Then I would say that you are trying to get free Doubles."

My parents did not have the legal knowledge to protect their intellectual property. Documenting the history of this national delicacy will at least recognize, though posthumously, the innovative husband-and-wife team of Emamool and Rasulan Deen for their creative vision, which continues to inspire many people to tap into their creativity to solve what may at first seem unsolvable personal challenges.

The story of Doubles is a case study in self-sufficiency, hard work, persistence, and determination to create one's own destiny when faced with daunting challenges that require pulling oneself up without a rope. The indomitable will of the first family of Doubles to nurture a vision and withstand the early ridicule, shame, and stigma is a living testament to Emamool and Rasulan Deen's unwavering courage to change the eating habits of a plural society. They achieved their objective through their compelling common sense and the positive choices they made. Their commitment and laser-like focus on perfecting their idea proved to be the winning formula in the introduction of a new street food to the nation.

Chapter 4:
The Childbearing Years

When Rasulan became pregnant with identical twin boys, her siblings Ding Ding, Babe, and Cassim were sent back to their father's house in Fairfield, since that household now had two daughters-in-law who could take care of the little ones. Unbeknown to Rasulan, MamooDeen was having an affair with a beautiful woman named Baby Abdul in the house opposite his on Bonanza Street where they lived. Baby Abdul was simultaneously pregnant with his child—also a boy—who was born January 12, 1937. The twins were born on February 28, 1937. The joke was that MamooDeen created triples as well as Doubles in Princes Town.

Bombay called the twins Nabi Baksh and Quda Baksh, unofficially passing on his surname of Baksh. Emamooldeen's surname should have been Baksh, but because of his imposed illegitimacy by the colonial powers, it was never recorded. Similarly, the twins, Habil and Cabil, were officially "illegitimate" and did not have last names on their birth certificates. The love child, Sabil, would later carry the name Hollis Adam Joseph from the maternal side of his family.

When illiterate Indian villagers went to the registrar to record the births of their newborns, it was an exercise in linguistic chaos. The non-Indian clerical personnel, for whom the English language was enough of a challenge, felt no obligation to attempt proper pronunciation of these low-status Hinglish-speaking Indians and invariably mangled their names. The imperfect communication often resulted in the dates of births being recorded incorrectly.

Also, since Hindu and Muslim newborns were classified as illegitimate, the father's names and surnames were excluded; if mentioned, they would be listed on the birth certificate as the informers of the birth.

Author's birth certificate describing him as illegitimate, with no surname; his father was listed as informant of the birth.

Rasulan's reaction to Baby Abdul was one of extreme loss of self-esteem and confidence in holding on to MamooDeen.

She knew she could not compete with the more beautiful, fair-skinned, glamorous, and urbanized rival.

Baby Abdul would "throw words" at Rasulan, saying that only animals produce children in litters, referring to the twins. She called Rasulan names, including *warahoon*—a primitive, unsophisticated Amerindian people.

The face-to-face competition on the same street made it unbearable, so Rasulan pleaded with MamooDeen to move back to the village of Fairfield, near her father and siblings, where she would be in her comfort zone. As luck would have it, they found out that a couple named Goojra and Rosie were selling their incomplete "house," located on the third housing lot on the southeastern side of the T-junction of Fairfield Road and Naparima Mayaro Road.

The Move to Fairfield

They bought the house shortly after the twins were born, in March 1937, for the grand total of ninety-six dollars from the profits of their new enterprise. The land consisted of two lots leased from the Fairfield Sugar Estate. The "house" was a wooden shack on wooden stilts, with a carat (thatch) roof and a wooden ladder for steps to enter the home—like the wooden ladders used by chickens to enter their coops.

They moved in with the twin babies. They were ridiculed for buying half of a house, but they were undeterred and focused on the vision of a whole house that would provide ample space on the western side for their first dedicated Doubles Kitchen. The back lot was used for a kitchen garden and the rearing of some cattle, goats, chickens, and ducks.

Rasulan's younger siblings were extremely happy to have her back in the village, within walking distance of their father's home. They spent most of their time with her and returned home only to sleep.

Rasulan also felt a sense of security living a few houses away from her maternal aunt Masitan, to whom she had gotten attached after losing her mother. Masitan became the surrogate maternal grandmother, "Nanee," to Rasulan's children. She played a very important role in our lives as the wise, resourceful, and generous grandmother and mentor. She was the first person Rasulan would call on with any problem she had. When we were ill, Nanee would be consulted first and would recommend some bush medicine. She was famous for her medicinal concoction called *zebapique*. The horrible taste of this bush medicine was guaranteed to cleanse the body of any ailment. The expression "bitter like zebapique" was commonly used in the village. Rasulan memorized the herbal formulae from Masitan and became quite adept at prescribing remedies for common ailments. She reciprocated Masitan's generosity by sending her daughters Hamidan and Sharm to help Masitan with her domestic duties.

Masitan was a single parent of six children: four sons, Abdul Aziz, twins James and John, and George; and two daughters, Intajan and Muntajan. James related in June 2010 that his mother originally named him and his twin brother Abdul Gafoor Mohammed and Abdul Satar Mohammed, but when they entered school, the headmaster, Mr. Espinet, thought their names were inconsistent with their multiracial features and influenced Masitan to change their names to James and John West.

Masitan was an independent pillar of strength for her six children. She owned a few cattle, goats, and chicken, and on her rented land she grew sugarcane and rice. She cultivated cash crops like *okro* (okra), *bodi* (string beans), *seime* (a flat bean), tomatoes, hot peppers, and ground provisions such as *eddoes*, sweet potatoes, cassava, corn, and so on. Her family subsisted off the land like most other villagers. To generate cash flow, she sold her produce from a wooden tray she carried on her head while holding in her hand a pail of fresh cow's milk that she also vended.

James West said his French Creole father, Albert West, and his mother focused his attention on education very early in his life with private lessons. His mother would remind him that education was his only escape from poverty. He did not disappoint them, as he went on to win scholarships to attend Presentation College in San Fernando and later the University of Manitoba in Canada, where he obtained his bachelor's and chartered accountant degrees. For James, John, and George, education was their ticket out of the harsh subsistence farming environment into which they were born.

Circumcision

In 1951, when I was six years old, Jamaloo was eight, and Shamal was four, we were circumcised according to Muslim rites. The man who performed the "surgery" was Mr. Aziz, known as "Clipper." He was a barber by trade and rode a bicycle. He was the most respected and feared man among Muslim boys. As a disciplinary threat, uncircumcised Muslim boys were told that if they misbehaved, Clipper would pay them a visit.

I recall the day of the circumcision, when the three of us had early baths and put on new, loose, pink gowns—with no underwear, of course. We were paraded in front of our family, uncles, aunts, and cousins. Some of our aunts gave us six-cent coins. Starting with Jamaloo, the oldest, we were each taken to the open veranda where the makeshift "operating theater" was set up.

As he had done with our twin brothers, who had endured the ritual about eight years before, my father took each of us in turn and sat us down at the edge of a low, wooden bench. He sat behind us to hold us still while Clipper clipped away with his barber's razor, which he sanitized over the flame of a lighted pitch-oil lamp. To keep us still, my father had a very effective technique: with our hands hung on the inside of our legs, he grabbed them from the outside of our legs, thereby simultaneously immobilizing our hands and legs, leaving us to the unanaesthetized mercy of Clipper. Without anesthesia, the surgery was painful. I still cringe when I think of the immediate stinging sensation.

When the surgeries were completed, we were placed in bed on our backs, and our pelvic areas were covered with flour. It was believed that flour was an antiseptic and a blood cauterant. Amazingly, we healed naturally and recovered from the traumatic experience.

Because of their cultural and religious persuasions, my parents did not conduct this practice to hurt or abuse us and so did not consider male circumcision as a form of child abuse or a human-rights violation.

Chapter 5: The Mobilization of Doubles

To transport his Doubles and Kripsy Chana, the creative and handy MamooDeen built a small wooden box to fit the tray on the rear of his Raleigh bicycle. The quantity of curried chana filled a five-pound baking-powder tin. That was a significant increase in quantity from the amount he had sold from the enamel bowl out of his hand basket. He secured the box to the bicycle's tray with wooden pegs through holes. He had such great pride in his products that when hopping onto his bicycle, he would not cross his leg over the food but instead would pull his foot, with great agility, over the bike's bar in front of him.

He pedaled his bike from Fairfield to Princes Town, his first sales territory, through winding, hilly, narrow, and rough roads that made the distance of 2.2 kilometers, or 1.37 miles, seem much longer. His Raleigh bicycle thus became the first mode of transportation to mobilize the Doubles business. When he reached Princes Town, he would park the bike in the raised triangular pavement in the center of the town and solicit his sales from there. They called this town center "the Square," even though it was a triangle.

Doubles were sold for six cents each, and Kripsy Chana was now a penny (two cents) a pack. Prices were tied to the denomination of the coins for ease of transaction. When sales started to exceed eight dollars per day, my parents thought they were becoming rich. The daily cash flow from their own enterprise provided them with immediate financial security that did not exist in the agricultural sector on which most villagers were dependent. They had in them the secret ingredient to a better economy and a better way of life and realized that they had a winner. They felt they had taken back their lives from the oppressive system, just like their grandparents had taken back their lives after indentureship.

Earning a living from agriculture was uncertain work that required great patience for a meager remuneration. That uncertain lifestyle could have been a contributing factor to the delayed-gratification characteristic of rural Indians. MamooDeen brought to Fairfield from Princes Town a new, nonagricultural way of earning a living that did not exist there before. The village community certified him as a qualified pioneer for his originality and independence.

MamooDeen had a new bilingual street cry: "Hot-hot-garam-garam." Garam means hot in Hindi. In Hindi, when the subject is plural, the adjective is sometimes repeated for emphasis and good expression. The intended subject was Doubles, which he did not vocalize in this street cry. His pronunciation of the word "hot" sounded more like "hat," and so the public would hear his street cry as, "Hat-e-hat-garam-garam."

The Doubles business continued to prosper and allowed my parents to complete the house with a comfortable front porch, or gallery, which was the most-used space of the house after the Doubles Kitchen. My grandfather Bombay moved in with them.

The Doubles Freight Bicycle

The "prosperity" also led to the purchase of the first freight bicycle—a bicycle with a built-in rectangular freight carrier in front and a smaller front wheel to accommodate the freight carrier. A built-in stand at the front of the carrier allowed for parking the bike on any flat surface.

On the handle bar of his freight bike, MamooDeen installed two melodious bells, which he would ring with both his thumbs, that produced a sustained sound while he held on to the bike handle. He also attached to the handle bar a rubber bulb trumpet horn, which he squeezed to produce a loud sound. These sounds, his broad-brimmed hats, and his colorful attire would complement his street cry of "hot-hot-garam-garam" and were effective in getting his customers' attention. His Doubles freight bike was his and his family's effective escape vehicle from the agrarian lifestyle of Fairfield.

Freight Bike

Trumpet Bulb Horn   **Melodious Bell**

MamooDeen's custom wooden box was fitted in the
cargo area of the freight bike. The freight bike and
trumpet bulb horn are originals.

The Doubles Box

MamooDeen, who was extremely handy and innovative, built a wooden box to fit the cargo area of the bicycle and created compartmentalized spaces for the curried chana, baras, chutney, and wrapping paper, as well as a space that served as a cash register to hold the coins. The curried chana was contained in a five-gallon vegetable-oil tin. The bara section of the box was lined by cloth recycled from flour sacks. These bara cloths would absorb the oil from the fried baras and also keep them moist and soft. Chutneys had their own smaller containers in the Doubles Box, which was covered with a vinyl material they called "oilcloth." The waterproof material had a shiny, colored vinyl side and a canvas-like underside. At the top front of the Doubles Box, the oilcloth was attached with a row of shiny chrome thumbtacks. The end to open the cover was attached to a round piece of wood, like a broom handle, to provide weight against the wind and for ease of opening the box. The top of the box was graded so the rain could easily run off.

This first Doubles Box was painted a brilliant yellow to represent the yellow curried chana inside and was the prototype for the ubiquitous Doubles Box, now in different colors, seen throughout Trinidad. Even when "Doublesmen" graduated from freight bikes to pickup vans and Doubles depots and outlets, they continued to use the Doubles Box, which remained the iconic product symbol for Doubles.

Shamal at Deen's Doubles Depot in 2005 using a wooden compartmentalized Doubles Box like MamooDeen's original design

The freight bike was a major improvement over Mamoo-Deen's Raleigh men's bike. It accommodated the larger cargo of Doubles that was now in demand. With its customized Doubles Box, the freight bike became the standard mode of transportation for Doubles.

The ingenious MamooDeen designed and built his house, his Doubles production kitchen, the Doubles Box, and all the tools of his new trade. He utilized used automobile leaf springs as burner grates across the firesides to hold the pitch-oil tins used for boiling the chickpeas. He straightened the curved leaf springs using the back of his axe as a sledgehammer. He made metal strainers to scoop out the boiled chana from the hot liquid. From the trunk of a hardwood tree, he shaped a large wooden mortar about three feet high and eighteen inches in diameter with a twelve-inch-deep cavity for processing the spices and ingredients used in the making of Doubles. At the striking end of the pestle, he fitted a two-inch metal ring. This ring added a cutting edge for faster processing. One of the ingredients that were daily crushed in the mortar was fresh hot congo peppers. The pepper residue was absorbed by the mortar's inner wooden surface and transferred to any ingredient processed in it. No amount of washing could eliminate the embedded capsaicin.

For the carnival celebrations in Princes Town, Mamoo-Deen anticipated the greater demand for his Doubles and built a large box-cart with metal wheels that transported more Doubles cargo than his freight bike could have carried. He dressed in very colorful carnival costumes and wore a sombrero. Only the boys in the family would accompany him, pushing this big box-cart to the town center almost two miles away. It was like our own Deen's Doubles float in the carnival parade. Catering to the happy carnival revelers was productive and remunerating fun for us.

Papa was a physically strong man who became stronger from riding his heavy freight bike over rough terrain. The ability to maneuver a front-heavy two-wheeler freight bike on rough terrain required great athletic skills and agility. The weight of the Doubles cargo in the front of the bike required Ma's assistance to hold on to the back of the bike as they guided it down the hill from the house to the road. Once on the saddle, Papa's weight provided the necessary equilibrium not to tip over. His physical strength was repeatedly demonstrated by the ease with which he could walk up the hill in front of the house with a hundred-pound sack of flour or chickpeas on his shoulder.

Every aspect of producing Doubles was labor-intensive, requiring strong bodies and stamina. It also required everyone, including the children, to help in the family business. The home-based family business instilled in us the importance of hard work and responsibility from an early age.

Waste Not, Want Not

The frugal Deen family, like most poor villagers, would never waste anything. For example, the five-gallon tin container for the vegetable oil, when emptied, would be recycled several times, never to be discarded. It was first used as a container for the curried chana in the Doubles Box. After that, it would be used as a pot for boiling the chana over the wood fire, then it would become a garbage can, and finally it would be cut and flattened out to cover the chicken-coop roofs.

Flour sacks were commonly used to make clothing for the family. Fancy bloomers were made for the girls by dyeing the fabric in the colors of their choice. In the absence of bassinets and cribs, Ma made small hammocks out of the flour sacks for her nine babies. The sacks were also cut and used as kitchen towels, *saapi* (potholders), and, as mentioned, bara cloths.

The jute bags the chana came in were used to transport agricultural produce and to make adult hammocks. Before they were finally discarded, they would also be used as doormats.

The unsold baras, if they were not eaten by the family, were soaked in water to feed to the chickens and especially the ducks, which loved them.

The highly nutritious stock from the boiled chana was used to feed their and Nanhoo's few cattle. Cassim would carry the stock in buckets for Nanhoo's cattle, but only after he first placed his hands in the stock, searching for any left-over grains of chana to eat. He would also drink a few hand-fuls of the stock before carrying the buckets home.

The Ali Brothers' Entry into the Doubles Business

Emamool Deen (sitting); standing left to right: Asgar Ali, Babwa Deen (Emamool's brother), and Choate Ali, circa 1940

When MamooDeen met Rasulan's brothers Asgar and Choate, they were charcoal salesmen. They produced and sold their charcoal using animal-drawn carts. Shortly after marrying MamooDeen's sisters, their charcoal venture came to an end when the owners of the lands where the charcoal was produced denied them further access. They were now unemployed while still living in their father's house with their wives. MamooDeen, the father figure to his sisters, devised a plan for his unemployed brothers-in-law.

The twins were ten months old when Rasulan was pregnant with Subrattan, the first daughter, who was born on October 7, 1938. During this pregnancy, my parents needed help in the Doubles business and with the infants Habil and Cabil. The problem solver that he was, MamooDeen made one decision that would solve both Rasulan's need for help and the unemployment of his two brothers-in-law. Having seen the opportunities and possibilities that Doubles offered, he selflessly invited them to experience his vision. He employed Asgar and Choate to sell his Deen's Doubles, and he got their wives, MamooDeen's two sisters, to help in production in the Doubles Kitchen.

MamooDeen stood security for the two freight bikes that Asgar and Choate first used to sell his Deen's Doubles. MamooDeen's design of his Doubles Box was duplicated for their two freight bikes. They made installment payments for the freight bikes from their wages. Asgar chose San Fernando, about nine miles from Fairfield, as his target market, but Choate decided there was no problem staying in Princes Town and selling Deen's Doubles to Mamoo-Deen's customers.

Asgar has related how on many occasions, both he and Choate returned to Deen's Doubles Kitchen at the end of the day with unsold Doubles. MamooDeen, the charismatic salesman that he was, would take the unsold products back to Princes Town to complete the day's sales. On returning, he would still pay them the agreed-upon compensation. Asgar's two sons, Doye and Mustapha, who inherited Ali's Doubles in San Fernando, have corroborated their father's recollection.

The employment arrangement would continue for several months until Asgar, Choate, and their wives learned the details and the secrets of the trade in MamooDeen's Doubles Kitchen. They were encouraged to start their own Doubles business with the blessings of MamooDeen and Rasulan because their independence would avoid future problems inherent in an extended-family business arrangement. MamooDeen saw their independence not as competition but as his reward for helping them to become productive and self-sufficient. His two sisters could now enjoy some economic security. He relied on a "moral noncompete agreement" and never thought that Asgar or Choate would want to compete directly with him in Princes Town. But in the case of Choate, he was wrong.

Rasulan described MamooDeen as the self-confident charismatic leader who took a leadership role to get things done in this extended-family relationship. She said Mamoo-Deen was the lead negotiator with Fairfield Sugar Estate to rent the four adjacent lots on the eastern side of his house— two lots each for Asgar and Choate—and helped negotiate the purchase of materials to build their houses in 1938–39.

The three north-facing houses were situated on their respective front lots facing the east–west Naparima Mayaro Road.

MamooDeen's track record as an assertive, independent entrepreneur generated confidence in his suppliers to extend him credit for the supplies he bought to produce Deen's Doubles. He advised his brothers-in-law about the microfinancing arrangement he had with these suppliers, which he called "making a turnover." It was a payment plan that paid off the previous balance before new credit was extended. In this way, he was never inundated with debt. This is not unlike the smart users of today's credit cards who pay off their monthly balances to avoid high interest rates and earn a good credit rating.

From their new houses, Asgar and Choate became independent of Deen's Doubles and launched their own brand: Ali's Doubles. It should be noted that when Asgar and Choate were selling Deen's Doubles produced in MamooDeen's Doubles Kitchen, there were no signs on the Doubles Boxes or freight bikes, so the consumer identified the brand by the salesman.

Asgar continued to develop the San Fernando area, where he started at Naparima College and then High Street, San Fernando. He later relocated his family from Fairfield to Vistabella in San Fernando to be nearer his target market. With the help of his two sons, Doye and Mustapha, he made Ali's Doubles the most successful Doubles brand in San Fernando and other locations.

Choate, however, decided to stay in Princes Town and compete with MamooDeen for the same customers. This was the origin of a cold relationship between our two families that would last through three generations.

MamooDeen's life of selfless cooperation and altruism left no room for greed and deceit. His character dictated that he could not indulge in ruthless competition with his own relatives. So when Choate decided to usurp Princes Town as his sales territory, MamooDeen, for the benefit of his sister, Choate's wife, saw bigger opportunities elsewhere. He saw the whole country as an untapped market.

Thus, from his Princes Town base location, he expanded his sales territory to the surrounding villages. On government and estate paydays, he loaded his Doubles Box into the trunk of a taxi and traveled eighteen miles to the Rio Claro town center, where he sold Deen's Doubles in front of a "rum shop." On other days, he would ride his freight bike to areas like Sainte Madeline, Barrackpore, Monkey Town, Buen Intento, and many other villages.

Testimonials about the Origin of Doubles

The oral history of the origin of Doubles was related by my parents, uncles, older siblings, cousins, and community elders who were either relatives or peers of my parents and custodians of these memories. I made video recordings of some of these eyewitnesses giving testimonials that corroborate the oral history that is being retold in this book.

When some local researchers write about the origin of Doubles, incomplete oral history leads them to Princes Town, where Doubles were created, but the identity of the pioneer eludes them. The factual blurring of the origin of Doubles is understandable, since the last time Deen's Doubles were sold by Emamool Deen and his twin sons, Habil and Cabil, in Princes Town was in 1957. The oldest brand name of Doubles currently sold there is Ali's Doubles. Also, the historical inaccuracy portrayed in the local media is not refuted by those wishing to usurp the pioneer status of Emamool and Rasulan Deen. In a documentary shown at the University of the West Indies, Saint Augustine, Trinidad, in October 2010 titled *Doubles with Slight,* even the academic researchers misrepresented the historical fact when they cited Ali's Doubles as the first brand.

Through hard work and dedication in promoting Doubles, Mustapha Ali became the largest-volume seller of Doubles in Trinidad. When he was interviewed on national TV about his success, he gratefully commended his uncle MamooDeen for starting the Doubles enterprise in 1936 in Princes Town and for bringing his father, Asgar Ali, into the business shortly thereafter.

On a video recording made at his beach house in Mayaro, Asgar's eldest son, Doye, who sells Ali's Doubles and other ethnic foods at his popular location in Vistabella, San Fernando, quoted his father as saying that "Mamoo-Deen wanted to make sure that his sisters were taken care of, so he brought his brothers-in-law, Asgar and Choate, into the business." Doye also stated, at his home and business place in a video recording on Doubles in October 2010: "For everything that I have and everything that you see here, I owe it to my uncle MamooDeen, who brought my father into the business." Doye's two sisters, Habiban and Halima, also recall with certainty the extended family's history that places their uncle, MamooDeen, as the one who created Doubles and who shared his vision with their father, Asgar, and uncle Choate.

In a video interview in the 1990s, Abdul Aziz, a first cousin of Rasulan, Asgar, and Choate, who for a short time sold Deen's Doubles for MamooDeen, paid special tribute to MamooDeen for his altruism and stated very emphatically that when it comes to the origin of Doubles, "It was Mamoo-Deen and MamooDeen alone, no partners, who brought Doubles to market."

Abdul Aziz's brother, eighty-year-old James West, who now resides in Montreal, Canada, stated clearly and without hesitation on June 24, 2013, that "the product Doubles, known by some as Bara and Chana, was created in Princes Town and brought to our village of Fairfield by Emamool Deen. This I am sure of. I have no question in my mind that the originator, the nucleus of Doubles, was Emamool Deen."

A next-door neighbor, eighty-five-year-old Sonny Mohammed, nicknamed Chone, was born August 31, 1928. He lived in Fairfield all his life and currently lives a few houses away from where MamooDeen and Rasulan lived and produced Deen's Doubles. He recalled vividly in May 2011 that "no one could come forward to say anyone but Mamoo-Deen started Doubles in Princes Town. MamooDeen was the founder of the Doubles business. MamooDeen brought the Doubles business to Fairfield, and any Fairfield villager from that time period would know the history of Doubles and know MamooDeen as the man who created it. I can prove this anywhere, and nobody can doubt me at all."

Sonny Mohammed's brother, seventy-eight-year-old Rafeek Mohammed, nicknamed Palmers, who was born July

1, 1935, grew up with MamooDeen's firstborn twins, Habil and Cabil, and James West. He stated in a video recording in May 2011 that the creator of Doubles was common knowledge in Princes Town. He said, "The first man I know in my lifetime to create and sell Doubles was MamooDeen." Palmers was also aware that MamooDeen started Deen's Doubles in Bonanza Street, Princes Town, before moving to Fairfield, next door to his family home.

Rahamat "Ding Ding" Ali, who was eighty-one years old when I interviewed him in 2009, was an eyewitness who spent a significant amount of time with his older sister, Rasulan, at her home and Doubles Kitchen. In the video interview, he stated, in the presence of Asgar's son Mustapha, who corroborated his statement, that it was unmistakably his brother-in-law, MamooDeen, who started the Doubles business and later employed his older brothers, Asgar Ali and Choate Ali, in the business. When Ding Ding relocated to Penal from Fairfield, he and his family also produced and sold Doubles for a living.

The eighty-five-year-old iconic politician Kamaluddin Mohammed, in May 2012, during an interview at his home in Mohammedville, El Socorro, recalled being introduced in the early 1940s to MamooDeen as the creator of Doubles by Mr. Bhaggirath Maharaj, who was married to MamooDeen's stepsister and was a prominent businessman in Princes Town. Mr. Mohammed said it was the first time he became aware of Doubles. He also recalled MamooDeen introducing Doubles to San Juan in the Croisée next to where his brother Joe Mohammed vended his fresh coconuts.

Seventy-nine-year-old Roodal Nandalal, who lives in Silvermill, San Juan, recalled on July 15, 2013, that he knew

MamooDeen sold his Doubles in the Princes Town Square in the early 1940s and was an eyewitness to the introduction of Deen's Doubles to San Juan and Port of Spain in the early 1950s. Roodal, as well as his mother, Stranger, and his six siblings were fruit and vegetable vendors in the San Juan Market. The family befriended the newcomer, MamooDeen. Roodal said Deen's Doubles was a strikingly new and unusual food product in the San Juan Market, and he was sure that any vendor in that market from that time could vouch for the fact that Deen's Doubles were the first Doubles to be sold in San Juan.

On January 27, 1995, during his presentation on Indian Arrival Day in Parliament, Mr. Mohammed Haniff, the parliamentary representative for Princes Town, posthumously recognized Raheman Rasulan Deen for creating Doubles in Princes Town. The Hansard that recorded this information on that date is the only official record of the origin of Doubles.

Astonishingly, when Choate, of Ali's Doubles in Princes Town, was interviewed on the local TV program *Cross Country* that was featuring Princes Town, we were all flabbergasted to hear his self-proclaimed pioneer status for creating Doubles in 1936! He made this claim a few years after the death of MamooDeen in 1979. The timeline leading up to Choate's launching of Ali's Doubles from his own house, which was built in 1938–39 is indisputable, making his and his family's claim null and void of credibility. Their claim to pioneer status does not stand the test of simple chronology. Also, when the sons of Asgar Ali, the older brother of Choate Ali, publicly proclaimed that it was their uncle

MamooDeen who created Doubles and introduced it to the Ali brothers (Asgar and Choate), it makes Choate's claim appear mischievous.

Thirty years after MamooDeen's death, on September 24, 2009, at an Eid Dinner organized by Congress of the People (COP) at the Motorway Building in Princes Town, Choate's family accepted a posthumous Certificate of Recognition on behalf of their parents, Choate and Rosidan, "for creating Doubles." In the audience witnessing this ceremony was Imam Sheikh Nazrudeen Mohammed, who knew the true story of the origin of Doubles. He said he was stunned by the falsehood being perpetuated in accepting this public recognition. In doing so, the Choate family had usurped the credit and truth that was due to MamooDeen and Rasulan. Most importantly, to intercept the credit is to distort the history of this national heritage.

My mother compensated for her illiteracy with a great memory and made sure, with repetition over the years, that the history of Doubles remains indelibly etched in our memories. In a video recording made in Winnipeg in response to Choate's false claim, she said in her broken English, "The truth does not 'out off,' a lie does 'out off.'" In other words, she was confident that the truth that is owed to Emamool and Rasulan Deen will prevail.

The Deen family not only created Doubles but spent decades creating the demand for Doubles in Princes Town, San Juan, Port of Spain, and Winnipeg, Canada. The Deens paved the way for easy entry to those markets by Choate's family, relatives, and others who benefited from the misfortunes of the Deens' early deaths in Trinidad and a divorce in

Winnipeg. It is said that imitation is the best form of flattery, but when the imitator ruthlessly usurps the credit due the imitated one, it only confirms a lack of originality. Mamoo-Deen's creativity, reputation, branding, and image of his entrepreneurial creation may be imitated but will never be duplicated.

Indira Gandhi aptly stated that "there are two types of people, those who create and those who take credit for what was created. It is better to be among the former because there is too much competition in the latter."

Chapter 6: Life on "Happy Hill"

As the years passed by, the three Doubles families would produce twenty-two children. MamooDeen and Rasulan had nine: six boys and three girls; Asgar and Kasidan had six: three boys and three girls; and Choate and Rosidan had seven: five boys and two girls. There were no fences between the houses, so the children had, in effect, one big yard in which to play. The innocent and cheerful voices of children playing at dusk every day brought comfort to the families at the end of their tiresome days. The big yard was known by the villagers as Happy Hill.

Toys

In our ethnic Muslim home in the late 1940s, Christmas was acknowledged but not celebrated. In retrospect, I wonder whether religion or my parents' economic situation was the reason we did not get toys for Christmas.

Our domestic animals were our real animated toys. Other toys were homemade. A toy train was made from sardine tins for carriages and a corned-beef tin for the engine, joined together with strings—wheels not included.

"Spinners" were made by flattening crown corks from soft-drink bottles. Two holes were punched out in the middle of the flattened disc through which a piece of string was threaded. The two ends of the string were tied together, forming a loop. With the disc in the middle of the loop, the string was held by both index fingers. With a little dexterity, you could get the disc to spin rapidly by pulling your index fingers in and out. The rapid speed of the spinner generated a buzzing sound. Mischievous boys would sharpen the edges of the discs and compete in cutting each other's strings in the game called "zwill."

My first "motorized" toy was made from a wooden bobbin. The two raised ends of the bobbin were cut in a serrated manner to imitate tire grooves and create traction. A rubber band was inserted through the hole and held together on one end with a piece of used wooden matchstick that was shorter than the diameter of the bobbin's sides so as not to restrict its movement. The matchstick was held in a carved-out groove on the side of the bobbin. On the other end was attached a longer piece of stick, such as a chopstick. Between the bobbin and the stick, a thin disc cut from a candle with a hole in the center was inserted to minimize friction. When the rubber band that held everything together was wound up and the bobbin was placed on the ground, it would move forward by rubber-band power.

We made kites using *cocoyea* (the ribs of the coconut leaves) to construct the skeleton of the kite, over which colorful tissue paper was stuck on with a paste made from flour and water. They were made in different styles and sizes. Two memorable styles were the "chickichong" and the "mad bull."

The chickichong was the simplest style, usually made from a copybook page without any skeletal support. The two vertical edges were folded back about an inch to provide some stability. A string was attached through two holes, one on top and the other at the bottom of the page where the kite's paper tail was attached. The main string was then tied to the string that was attached to the kite, and it was now ready for flight.

The mad-bull kite was for older children and adults. It was made from sturdier materials, and once in the air, it required greater dexterity to maneuver. The mad bull's unique feature was the roaring sound it made. At the top of the kite was a raised bow. Along the string of the bow a folded strip of tissue paper was attached with flour paste, and this "tongue" would flap in the wind, creating the sound of the colorful mad bull.

We loved "rolling rollers," utilizing any used wheel or sturdy tire that children—especially boys—would roll on the ground by hand or with a stick. The best rollers were bicycle rims without the spokes and hub. A round stick was used in the groove of the rim for acceleration and maneuverability. With the right technique and dexterity, we rolled rollers even on rough surfaces to keep them in constant motion. The physical exercise of running behind these rollers and playing outdoors in general eliminated any possibility for the obesity scourge experienced by inactive children playing video games nowadays.

We played cricket, learned from the British on the island, on any available level ground surface that could simulate a cricket pitch. We made bats from coconut branches, and the balls were shaped from the bulbous root of the bamboo plant. The improvised wicket was any piece of board or a small piece of corrugated galvanized metal propped up with a stick.

"Bussing bamboo" is a technique of creating a loud, explosive sound from a homemade cannon created from a large piece of bamboo. A six-foot length of bamboo with a diameter of about six inches is used to make this explosive sound device. All the bamboo's inner joints except an end joint are hollowed out. Near the closed end joint, a small hole is made. A small amount of pitch oil is poured into this end, with the other, opened end elevated. A lighter made of a small stick dipped in the pitch oil and lit from the flames of a flambeau is used to ignite and heat up the pitch oil in the bamboo and to trigger the explosion from the residual vapor after the smoke is blown out by mouth. Blowing out the smoke after each explosion has caused many accidents when the pitch oil in the bamboo was still on fire. Many eyebrows and eyelashes were singed in the process of bussing bamboo.

Bussing bamboo, with its loud reverberating sounds, was done at nights during the holiday seasons to disturb the nocturnal silence of the villages. There was much joy and laughter as we enjoyed playing with the fire and loud explosions. It was like hearing only the sound in a fireworks display without seeing the spectacular visuals.

We made our slingshots from small, Y-shaped tree branches and pieces of bicycle inner tubes attached to the tip of the Y-frame, and the pocket (*basil*), in which the projectile/bullet is placed, was made from pieces of leather from old shoes.

Playing with these homemade toys gave us not only joy but a deeper sense of pride of ownership, because we had created them.

Alcoholism and Domestic Abuse

When disposable income allowed the three Doublesmen to indulge in their vices, however, Happy Hill would lose its happiness to competition, alcoholism, domestic violence, and early deaths. For MamooDeen and Rasulan, Happy Hill became the hill of sorrows where indelibly sad memories continue to haunt their posterity.

Physical abuse was very common in Indian households in the rural villages of Trinidad in the 1930s and 1940s. Although there is no excuse or justification for the physical abuse endured by rural Indian women, scholars have cited the disparity between numbers of Indian men and women from the preceding indentureship scheme. Significantly fewer women than men came as indentured laborers, causing insecurity and jealousy among the men in their competition for the women's attention. That, the scholars say, led to the abuse.

The indenture system of subservience denied the laborers— especially the males—their self-pride, their self-esteem, and even their manhood. Those who were not subservient to the British slave masters/drivers were physically beaten into submission. Their worth to the sugarcane plantations was measured by their physical strength, which was their only asset of value.

After experiencing authority exercised with physical force by the colonial masters and their agents, some of the indentured laborers must have internalized the effectiveness of this form of authority to overcome any resistance. They would then use it in their only position of authority—over their own wives and children, whom they totally dominated and in whom they instilled fear to maintain control.

When poverty and illiteracy were combined with an oppressive work environment, displaced aggression on one's own family became par for the course. When alcohol was added to the mix, many families were destroyed or severely traumatized. The outlet for this suppressed rage manifested in the prevailing behavioral pattern of settling seemingly insignificant arguments with physical force.

In 1918 the Caroni Sugar Factory started to distill rum from sugarcane. Other sugar factories throughout the island would later distill rum as well. The production of sugarcane, which was the mainstay of the economy, provided an abundantly cheap supply of raw material for the rum industry. Rum was sold to the ubiquitous "rum shops" in bulk, where it was retailed inexpensively in "petit quarts" to their male clientele.

Rum and the Indian male in rural Trinidad makes for an interesting sociological study. Some researchers argue that capitalists used alcohol to suppress the working class. The original affinity that many Indian males had to rum may be explained by the nature of their employment. The Indian man in rural Trinidad had a significant input in producing the main ingredient in the rum-making process: sugarcane. He invested his blood, sweat, and tears—in fact, his life—in the production of sugarcane, and he felt entitled to partake in the fruits of his labor. Rum, a by-product of his physical strength, was a national product that he helped to create, and at the end of a physically hard day's work in the cane fields, it was rum time! He could not be deprived of this simple pleasure that temporarily gave him some escape from the rigors of his physical toil by numbing his senses to the oppressive system he had to endure.

As excessive consumption of alcohol became a habit, rum became the devil incarnate to so many families that would lose their loving and responsible husbands, fathers, and sons to this spirit in a bottle, which brought much despair and unhappiness to the communities.

Rum was the catalyst in most domestic violence in the Indian families of rural Trinidad. MamooDeen, Asgar, and Choate became drinking buddies, and their families were not spared the abuse from their drunken stupors. Under the influence of rum, MamooDeen became self-destructive, transforming into an errant husband and father.

Choate was our bellicose uncle who instilled fear and trauma in us, especially when he was under the influence of alcohol. One night while he was drinking with Papa at our home, he touched my sister Subrattan inappropriately, and when Habil intervened to protect her, Choate grabbed him by the scrota and would not let go. Papa, seeing Habil in agony, pulled Choate away and bodily threw him out of the house into the yard, where we had water barrels near the eaves. In one of the barrels was a loose galvanized spouting to help collect the rainwater. Choate's hand caught the spouting's sharp edge before he hit the ground, causing a large gash in his forearm. He went home with a bleeding arm but returned soon afterward with a cutlass, banging at the closed doors.

We were all holding Papa back from going outside, because if we didn't, there would have been a murder committed that night. After awhile Choate departed, and the traumatic experience subsided.

Another incident in which Choate terrorized our home occurred when we became the first family of the three to own a transistor radio powered by dry-cell batteries. Papa was not home at the time, and Choate, in his drunken state of mind, did not want us to enjoy the music on the radio. He started to pelt stones at our house while shouting obscenities. We quickly closed the doors and windows and ran to Ma for cover, like ducklings running under their mother's protective wings.

Ma related to us the many times Papa physically abused her while he was under the influence of alcohol. The last incident of physical abuse she would retell over the years, which remained vivid in the Deen household memory, occurred in 1944 when Shamedan was just a baby. Papa had returned home from a weekend of partying with rum, women, and song and found out from his father, Bombay, that Ma had left the house with some of the children to visit her sister Syde in Williamsville and left no cooked food for Bombay.

MamooDeen, stale-drunk and full of guilt from his joyous weekend escapade, listened to his father's complaints of Rasulan and, using his leather belt, proceeded to physically abuse her. His father supervised the abuse, advising him to "hit where it leaves no marks." In an attempt to avoid the blows, Ma tripped and fell into a canal of stagnant, black, fetid water on the side of the road in front of the house. She described the contents of the canal as soothing to the sting of the blows she'd received. When the abuse was over, as if possessed by some supernatural power, she went after her father-in-law, Bombay, the instigator of her abuse. She threw all his personal belongings out of the house and evicted him. She told him to go and live with his daughters.

Nanhoo came to see his battered daughter and told MamooDeen with intense sarcasm: "Why didn't you kill her? Death would have been less painful for her." He continued, "Don't forget that you have three daughters, and someday you will feel the pain I feel today." These words or curses, or *saraape* from the Hindi word *sharapna,* proved prophetic; none of the three girls would escape physical and verbal abuse from their husbands as soon as the novelty of their marriages wore off and familiarity and male dominance entered their marriages. My three sisters endured the physical and verbal abuse believing that it was their "cross to bear" from the *sara-ape* that our grandfather placed on Papa.

The plight of my uneducated peasant mother in a rural village in the 1940s, saddled with six children at the time, with no skills or material resources to pursue self-determined independence, was indeed daunting. She could not even take refuge at her father's home or with relatives because she would have been a great burden to their already meager existence. There was no support system, no home for battered women. Domestic violence was commonplace and accepted by society at the time.

When we asked Ma why she took the abuse and did not fight back, she would say that she was "illiterate but not stupid"—she wanted to live for her children. She told us of the time when she did consider murdering our father when he was drunk and had physically abused her. He was sitting on a bench with his head hanging toward his knees, falling asleep. She thought it was the opportune moment to use a sharp cutlass to behead him, but the thought of such a gruesome act shook her out of her temporary insanity. What she could not cure she had to endure. She, like my three sisters after her, felt the weight of her poverty and illiteracy under the rigid cultural expectations of the rural Indian village that demanded her silence, obedience, and endearing servility, even as a victim of domestic abuse.

The abusive marriage, in a strange way, was protecting her from an even harsher world that awaited her outside. To stay put was the lesser of the two painful options and in fact was her only choice. She had to resign herself to a life with a physically and verbally abusive husband for her mere survival and that of her children.

Ma, like a hostage experiencing the Stockholm syndrome—the psychological tendency of a hostage to bond, identify, or sympathize with his or her captor—experienced a resigned attachment to Papa and identified with his plight of creating his own space to provide sustenance for his family.

The family structure placed her in a condition similar to indentured servitude. Her only escape was in her prayerful hopes and dreams that with extreme patience of deferred gratification, someday her children, when grown, would take better care of her than her abusive husband had. She was living her life through her children and taught her three daughters to do the same.

The Twins: Habil and Cabil

Habil, left, and Cabil, right, 16 years old in 1953

The twins, Habil and Cabil, were the treasures of the Deen household. They were MamooDeen and Rasulan's own princes of Princes Town. Rasulan's relationship with them was unique, compared with the rest of her nine children. Because of her tender age at the time of their birth, she and the twins, in a sense, grew up together like siblings—another reason they called her *Daye,* or sister. The special bond she had with them was not replicated with the rest of us. A large family of nine like ours had subgroupings of interactions. The older children had their own group, as did the younger ones; but the subgroup of Ma and the twins was so special that even Papa became envious of them. Her loving relationship with the twins was the only power Ma had over Papa's dominance.

When the twins were about four years old, Ma was picking pigeon peas with them in her kitchen garden near the neighbor's property. In a split second, Cabil went missing, and panic broke loose. He had stepped on a rotted piece of wood that covered the neighbor's old cesspit, and he fell into it. She said she saw bubbles coming out of the fetid liquid and instinctively reached in and pulled her drowning baby out of the mess and resuscitated him. The incident caused a long-lasting rift between them and the neighbor for his negligence.

The neighbor, Geera, felt no remorse for his negligence and instead of apologizing, retaliated one day when Papa was using Geera's yard as a shortcut to tote a heavy sack of flour on his shoulders. Geera was a professional stick fighter with great skill. He struck Papa with one of his fighting sticks and warned him not to trespass on his property again. Papa took the blow and continued with his sack of flour to deliver it to the Doubles Kitchen. In the eave of the carat roof of the Doubles Kitchen, he kept his "brushing cutlass"—a scythe-like grass-cutting tool made from the old blade of a cutlass inserted in a slit and wired in place in the natural crook of the long handle cut from the hardwood guava tree. This tool was used together with a thinner "crook stick" that would part the grass before the user swiped it with the brushing cutlass.

Papa pulled out his hardwood brushing cutlass and went after Geera, who was still at the boundary line swearing at him. Geera, with his "stickmanship" and astounding agility, skillfully defended himself from the blows aimed at his head and body until Papa's blade broke off from the handle of the brushing cutlass. A real stick fight ensued, with both fighters displaying impressive martial arts dexterity. The combat ended in a fistfight on the ground, but not before Papa's sister Kasidan entered the fray and threw a few blows of her own at Geera. Had he not been such a great stickman, Geera would have been a casualty of Papa's brushing cutlass. Luckily, the only loss was their relationship.

The police took them into custody and obtained their statements. A court date was set for the hearing. Papa's father, Bombay, prepared some sort of a talisman for him to wear in his right shoe during the court appearance. When Geera came before the magistrate, he was confused and did not answer any questions; instead he just stood there and yawned. The magistrate dismissed the case, and my parents and grandfather were convinced it was the talisman that made Geera dumbfounded. James West vividly remembers this duel and recalls that for several days after the fight, Geera had his head wrapped in a bandage, which he tried to cover with his hat.

While in elementary school, the twins were very playful and fun loving but very mischievous. They sought refuge with our grandfather Bombay, whom they endearingly called Haji Baba. He would let them stay with him when they did not feel well enough to attend school and treated them with sweetened condensed milk.

Our half brother, Sabil, lived in our home intermittently and helped create even more mischief. As a team, the three of them did not lose their fights with other boys, so the complaints would always end up at MamooDeen's home. He would not hesitate to punish them without question and never gave them the benefit of the doubt.

Rasulan displaced the animosity she had for Baby Abdul to Sabil. Problems would arise with him, and he would run away back to his mother on Bonanza Street. Rasulan obviously showed preference for her twins over Sabil.

On one of Sabil's stays with the family, the three boys somehow obtained the lead from old batteries, melted it, and poured the hot liquid into bamboo forms, then cut the hardened lead into smaller pieces for use in their slingshots as bullets. This got them into major trouble when they shot a neighbor's cow in the eye with one of those lead bullets. When the complaint reached home, MamooDeen, intoxicated from drinking with his brothers-in-law, gave the three of them the flogging of their lives, with pieces of sugarcane used as whips. When the beating stopped, he hog-tied and hung them from the roof of the cow shed, left them there, and went back to drinking with Choate and Asgar.

Hamidan recalled that she and Subrattan went to see them strung up in the cowshed and tried to push their bodies up to minimize the weight on their tied hands and feet. MamooDeen returned sometime later in his drunken state to release them. Bombay tried to provide them some comfort by rubbing their bruises with ghee. Rasulan dared not intervene for fear of being physically abused also. When he was under the influence of alcohol, my father's feelings toward his family became more authoritarian and callous.

Another corporal punishment the twins received occurred after they got new school bags made of a heavy canvas material similar to military bags. They decided to "make l'ecole biche"—skip school without parental or teachers' permission. These young truants decided to go swimming in a muddy river and somehow got their school bags wet, which became the evidence of their truancy. After their punishment they were taken out of school, bringing to an end their formal education at the fifth standard level—sixth grade in the North American school system.

In their early teens, the twins started to experiment with liquor, and Habil showed a preference for Scotch whiskey and CC-Mel, a chocolate drink that camouflaged the taste but not the potency of the whiskey. They were following the example set by our father and uncles and felt that the consumption of alcohol was a rite of passage to manhood. Luckily, they did not abuse alcohol to the point of getting drunk and addicted.

It Takes a Village

Corporal punishment was the disciplinary norm for delin-
quent children at home, in school, or in public. It was
acceptable for parents, older relatives, neighbors, and even
strangers to discipline other folks' children as well, oftentimes physically, when they misbehaved.

People had confidence in the village community to look
after all its children. We had the freedom to drift away from
home without our parents knowing our whereabouts. In 2006,
Hillary Clinton called for the collective responsibility for raising
all of our children in her book *It Takes A Village*. In the early
1950s, the village of Fairfield was already raising all its children.

Between the ages of six and twelve, we had the freedom to
leave home for hours and relied on nature to provide us with treats
like mangoes and sugarcane. When the fruits were not within our
reach we pelted them with stones, developing our abilities to pitch
our cricket balls at the same time. We peeled these treats with our
teeth. Peeling sugarcane by teeth and sucking its juice required
hand and mouth coordination that developed the jaw muscles
and cleaned our teeth simultaneously. The dripping juices of these
treats would run down our arms, and we would lick them from
our elbows up to the palms of our hands. We wiped our mouths
with the backs of our hands or our shirtsleeves. We would return
home safely at dusk, like chickens coming home to roost.

Superstitions

Habil and Cabil enjoyed playing cricket. An incident that
remains vivid in my memory was when Habil got hit with

a cricket bat by a young man named Boyie. During an argu-
ment in playing the game, Boyie struck Habil on his head
with his bat. Habil became temporarily unconscious from
the blow. I recall an icepack being placed on his head, and as
with most injuries in the village, alternative "bush" medicine
and spiritual healing were their first recourse; only when all
alternative treatments were exhausted would medical help be
sought. Habil recovered from the blow to his head without
any medical doctor's intervention.

In addition to their religious beliefs, most villagers were
superstitious and believed in "bush" (herbal) medicine, spiritual
healing, casting spells, and exorcising "jumbees" (spirits) from
the possessed. Embedded in the fabric of Trinidadian daily lives
was the rich folklore from the many cultures and traditions
that have influenced its heritage: Spanish, French, African, and
Indian. From the mythical melting pot came popular, powerful tales that endured over time. Folklore characters—such
as *La Jablesse* or *La Diablesse,* the devil woman; *soucouyant,* the female vampire; *Lagahoo,* the shape-shifting were-
wolf; *Douen,* the spirit of a dead, unbaptized child; and *Papa
Bois,* the forest keeper, said to roam in the darkness of the
midnight hour—were powerful, creative imaginations that
scared us and the village youths from straying at night.

The myth of the *soucouyant* was the most intriguing for
me. It told of an old wrinkled-skin witch who had the power
to peel off her skin, place it in a mortar, turn into a ball of fire,
and fly from house to house to suck the blood of her victims.
The myth was especially scary to me because Miss Rollee, who
lived across the road in front of us, was labeled a soucouyant.
She was a gentle old lady who lived alone in an old wooden

house that 'time painted' a grayish-black. The roof of her house was made of corrugated, galvanized metal, on which mischievous boys would pelt stones to retaliate against their fear of her and her ascribed powers. The loud noise from the stones raining down on her galvanized roof greatly terrified poor Miss Rollee. Her complaints to the neighbors fell on deaf ears because they all believed the myth that she was a soucouyant.

My mother learned from her aunt Masitan to sprinkle salt around the house to protect us from the soucouyant whenever Miss Rollee came to pick up or deliver my father's clothes that she was given to iron. It was believed that when the soucouyant tried to enter a victim's house at midnight and encountered salt, she had to count all the grains of the salt before she could get in to suck your blood. By the time she had finished counting the grains of salt, it would be approaching daybreak, and she would have to hurry to get back into her skin before sunrise, thereby saving you the horrible experience of having your blood sucked by a soucouyant. It was also strongly believed that to destroy a soucouyant, you must first find her skin in the mortar and marinate it in salt and hot pepper. She would then be unable to reenter her pickled skin and would die in the light of day. No one ever found the skin of a soucouyant.

Poor Miss Rollee, who smoked a tobacco pipe, had no teeth. She made a living by washing and ironing people's clothes. She told my mother that her left hand was chopped off above the wrist by her jealous husband when the white plantation overseer showed interest in her. In attempting to protect her head from the blow of her husband's cutlass, she lost her hand.

Subrattan

Subrattan circa 1968

Born on October 7, 1938, Subrattan was the third—after the firstborn twins—of the nine Deen children and the first girl. She was the "most beautiful baby" in the village, having inherited the fair-complexioned gene from her father. Skin color always played a part in assessing beauty; people believed that the lighter the complexion, the more beautiful the person. Subrattan was her father's favorite.

Her schooling, which started at age five in 1943, ended when she turned thirteen in 1951. She had completed standard five (grade six). She was a bright student who showed great potential to become a scholar, but cultural norms would deny her any educational opportunities.

Just after her thirteenth birthday, she entered puberty, which meant in the prevailing culture that she was capable of bearing children, and the institution of marriage was a better protector against unwanted pregnancies than any institution of formal education. A pregnancy out of wedlock was such a social stigma that parents would sacrifice the innocence of their underage daughters to avoid the shame.

The deeply rooted cultural traditions and religious norms took precedence over nurturing her to live up to her full human potential. Her highest qualification was being a virgin at marriage. Her destiny, like her mother's, would be years of domestic duties and child rearing. No consideration was given to the fact that she was not ready mentally, emotionally, or physically to engage in sexual activity that would force her into early pregnancy. The lyrics from the 1980 philosophical calypso "Progress" by King Austin ring true for young Subrattan: "children making children."

The notion of consent was nonexistent, as she was too young to have her own views but old enough to have marriage imposed on her. She was not taught any life skills and lacked any knowledge of reproduction and contraception. She was being led into child marriage like a sacrificial lamb. These religious and cultural norms persisted because they were not challenged and took on an aura of morality in the village community. Opposition to child brides was not heeded. Subrattan stayed at home awaiting the fateful and still unknown wedding day, when she would marry someone who was equally unknown to her. She was forever denied a self-determined life, which was not seen as a human-rights abuse.

Mr. Jessimy, the school principal, begged our father not to take her out of school at such a tender age, but his plea fell on deaf ears. On his sales trips to Rio Claro, Papa had by then arranged with the parents of a boy named Mohammed "Dood" Ali, from Ecclesville, Rio Claro, for the marriage of his first and favorite daughter.

Dood, who was born May 11, 1936, was also just a kid of sixteen years when the arranged marriage was being planned. He and Subrattan were married April 6, 1952, in a Muslim wedding to which, as was customary, the whole village was invited. A huge tent was constructed with bamboo and covered with tarps. There was the typical abundance of Indian cuisine, such as large wedding *parathas*—a flat bread cooked by firewood on a large round grill called a *tawa* during the "cooking night" the night before the wedding. In the early morning of the wedding, the rest of the food items were cooked so that the guests and the groom's entourage— the *baraat*—would enjoy piping hot food. The meat of choice at a Muslim wedding was curried goat. Many goats were *halaled*— slaughtered under Muslim religious rites—for the auspicious event. There was also rice; *dhal*, yellow split-pea soup used as gravy on the rice; *chana and aloo*–curried chickpeas with potatoes, and mashed spicy pumpkin. Dessert was crispy *kurma*—deep-fried, flavored, bite-sized dough covered in sugar syrup and dried.

My indelible memory of Subrattan as a bride, *dulahin,* in a truly innocent white satin bridal gown with a pattern of eyelets throughout, is more powerful than any photograph that could have been taken had there been cameras in the village. These eyelets most appropriately represented the wide-opened eyes of Subrattan and the other child brides of the village, staring blankly at society's norms and not having the right to even ask why. The groom, *dulha,* wearing a turban, was equally innocent and depended on his parents and village elders to determine his destiny. The power of cultural traditions reigned supreme and produced its own morality in social contracts that gave consent to marriages of underage girls.

As was the custom, the newlyweds moved in with the groom's parents and siblings in Ecclesville, Rio Claro. Dood had four siblings: three sisters and a brother, who lived at home with them. His parents, Rahamut and Isha, were landowners who produced cocoa, coffee, dasheen (a variety of taro root), citrus, and other crops. Dood helped his parents in their agricultural activities, and Subrattan helped out with the domestic duties. The pattern of interpersonal relationships in her new extended family was complex. As was the custom, she had to be subservient not only to her husband but to his parents as well. As the novelty of their marriage wore off, Dood began to exert his male dominance over Subrattan and started the physical and verbal abuse that would last throughout her lifetime.

Nine months after her marriage, on January 21, 1953, Subrattan, the child bride at thirteen, was now a mother at fourteen. Her first baby, Jeniffer, was born at our home in Fairfield. Subrattan luckily survived the cultural Russian roulette that was played with her life at such an early age: the World Health Organization advises that child brides are five times more likely to die in childbirth at thirteen than at twenty years old. She only had a lactation problem and was spared the other severe complications experienced by young mothers of her age. Our mother, who luckily was still nursing Edool at two years old, filled Subrattan's lactation void and breast-fed her first granddaughter, Jeniffer, as well.

Music

Papa was a versatile singer and self-taught musician capable of playing his musical instruments by ear. He played the harmonium, *dholak,* and *dhantal.* He would take these instruments along with him to weddings and house parties and perform alongside the best local talents available at the time. His accompanying dholak player and friend was Cyril the "oyster man," who sold oysters in the same triangle in Princes Town where Papa sold his Doubles. Cyril would place a ring on his right index finger to create a pleasant-sounding rim shot on the high-pitched side of the dholak.

Papa's voice was sweet, melodious, and powerful. His street cries certainly contributed to the power of his voice, which did not require a microphone when he sang. While playing the harmonium, he sang a variety of ancestral song genres that were brought from India, such as *thumri, telana, qasidas, marphat gazals, hori, durphad, qawali,* and *chaiti*— songs that were the precursors of today's popular chutney music, which is a fusion with soca music. My mother would relate jealously that he sang and played music for the famous dancers Champa Devi and Alice Jan. His musical and singing contemporaries were Ball Bagai, K. B. Singh, Mosquito, Jagroo Kawal, and Taran Persad, among others.

His singing and musical abilities would charm his female fans, who would compete for his attention. His flamboyant attire, shoulder-length hair, and four gold rings on the fingers of his left hand, which bellowed the harmonium as he sang, appealed to his many admirers. He was without doubt a ladies' man. He would leave his family at home to attend Indian weddings that typically lasted a few days. He was not only the entertainer but the master chef who took charge of the preparation and cooking of the large quantities of food to serve the hundreds of guests. At these weddings, the public was usually invited. Papa would return home eventually to recuperate from the exertions of his sojourn. When Ma asked about his whereabouts, it invariably led to his verbal abuse of her.

Flamboyant MamooDeen with long hair

Papa taught the twins to play the musical instruments and to sing. Habil sang and played the harmonium, and Cabil, who also sang, played the dholak. With Papa on the dhantal and singing, they had a full family band. The sound of music would reverberate throughout the house and travel in the balmy breezes to entertain the neighbors as well.

Music brought the family happiness and escape from the busy schedule of the Doubles business. It brought the twins and their father closer, and his authoritative mannerism and emotional disengagement would dissolve when they made music together. Music also helped them develop their self-esteem and confidence to celebrate their independence from forces that dominated the lives of other villagers.

Learning Indian music followed the oral traditions from India, and like learning one's native language, one listened to other singers and musicians to learn the art. The twins would see Indian movies in the cinema and learn the songs instantly. They displayed remarkable musical talent and aptitude for children who had no television, radio, gramophone, or other exposure to music. Their music teacher was their multitalented father.

On one of his return trips to Fairfield from San Juan, Papa heard that Habil had taken the harmonium to a *maticoor*—the celebratory Saturday night before a Hindu wedding. Habil received rave reviews for his debut singing and harmonium playing, talents he learned from Papa. Instead of being happy with Habil's musical accomplishment, our intoxicated father became angry and proceeded to destroy the harmonium and dholak with the axe used for chopping firewood. He then placed all the broken pieces of the musical instruments into the fireside and burned them to ashes.

Putting an axe to a delicate instrument like the harmonium was a mind-numbing experience to witness. The whole family looked on in dismay and sadness at the destruction of these musical instruments that had brought us so much joy and happiness. The music played on those instruments had brought the twins and Papa closer together and created the missing visible bonding that we all longed for from an undemonstrative dad. The beautiful music and the ambience it created in the family literally went up in smoke.

Maybe he was insecure about seeing the twins excel in music, which had made him a popular singer/musician. But my mother was ambivalent about the loss of those instruments. If music was the food of love, as Shakespeare wrote, she would have been traumatized, but in her life, music became the catalyst for losing her loved ones to the pleasures of the world, so it was easier for her to accept the destruction of the musical instruments. This also seemed to have been Papa's motive in not wanting his sons to follow in his musical footsteps, which had led him astray and brought pain and misery to the family.

Papa realized that the absence of music in the family created a void that was like the loss of a loved one. He felt guilty for depriving us of the only pastime that the entire family enjoyed together—the joy of music. Several months later, on one of his return trips from San Juan, he bought a new harmonium and dholak. The joy of having the sound of live music return to the household warmed the hearts of the family, especially the twins. They sat on the floor with Papa and played the new instruments and sang with the joy of playing with new toys on a Christmas morning.

Dhantal

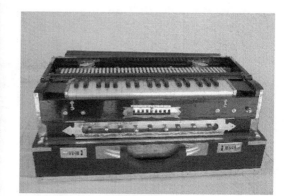

Harmonium

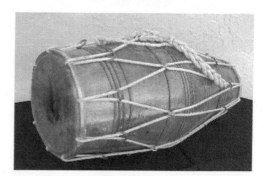

Dholak

The dhantal is a percussion instrument made from a resonating quarter-inch tempered-steel rod that is curved at the end that rests on the floor and tapered on the other end. A U-shaped piece of metal that fits in one hand is used to strike the vertical rod. The other hand is used to mute the rod for various percussive effects and to accentuate rhythms played. Its timbre is sharply metallic and provides a clearly defined *tal* (beat or pulse) to help the ensemble stay in rhythmic sync.

Some Trinidadian dhantal enthusiasts claim that the dhantal was created in Trinidad, but the fact that it still exists in the state of Bihar, India, today refutes that claim. Surinamese Pandit Stanley Bramhatiwari, who now resides in Miami, Florida, bought his dhantal in Mazaffarpur, Bihar, India, where his ancestors originated. Also, the fact that similar dhantals are used in Fiji, Guyana, and Surinam would suggest that it originated in India and was re-created in these countries, where the Indian diaspora settled in large numbers after indentureship.

A classical North Indian percussion instrument, the dholak is a two-sided hand drum. It is barrel-shaped with a simple membrane, usually goatskin, on the high-pitched side. The bass head is also made with goatskin, but a special material is applied to the inner surface. This material is a mixture of tar, clay, and sand called *dholak masala*, and it lowers the pitch and provides a well-defined tone that the accomplished player can bend. The drum's heads are tightened by pulling a series of metal rings and cords or using metal turnbuckles. Following the designs from India, woodworking artisans in Trinidad crafted their own dholaks.

The harmonium is a freestanding keyboard instrument similar to an accordion. Sound is produced by air blown through sets of free reeds by hand-operated bellows. Its sound is richer, deeper-sounding, and less abrasive than that of the accordion. It was invented in Paris in the mid-nineteenth century by Alexandre Franco Debain, who patented the name harmonium in 1842.

During the mid-nineteenth century, missionaries brought French-made, hand-pumped harmoniums to India. The instrument quickly became popular there because it was portable, reliable, and easy to learn. It has remained popular to the present day and is an important instrument in many genres of Indian music. The instrument was quickly adopted by Indians because Indian music is melodically based, and only one hand is necessary to play the melody, while the other hand is free for the bellows. It is commonly found in Indian homes. From the designs developed in France, the harmonium was developed further in India in unique ways, such as the addition of drone stops and a scale-changing mechanism. Unlike the dholak and dhantal that were subsequently made in Trinidad, harmoniums are still imported into Trinidad from India.

Chapter 7: MamooDeen's Vision for the Future of Doubles

After Asgar and Choate became independent of Papa, sales revenue from Doubles obviously decreased, going from three salesmen to just himself. Papa got Aziz, the eldest son of Ma's aunt Masitan, involved in the Doubles business. He included Aziz because he saw the endless potential for the business and also because Aziz's wife was his cousin whom he wished to help. Aziz did not have the passion for sales and soon returned to his agricultural endeavors.

Papa's dream of expanding the business was now focused on his own six sons, in whom he saw his family's security and the future possibilities for Doubles. He envisioned a Doubles empire in which he and his six sons would play the leading roles. Even though he was burdening his sons with his dreams, he was convinced that being one's own boss was the greatest achievement for a man, and he instilled this belief in his children. His belief echoes the words of the Bhagavad Gita, chapter 18, verse 47: "Greater is thine own work, even if this be humble, than the work of another, even if this be great. When a man does the work that God gives him, no sin can touch this man."

The Twins Join the Doubles Business

In the early 1950s, the twins, Habil and Cabil, started to help Papa sell Doubles in the Princes Town Square. This was actually on-the-job training for them to become Doublesmen. Habil soon replaced our father in his Princes Town base, leaving Papa free to explore new territories to expand the business. For a brief stint, Cabil had worked in the Craignish estate tending to field animals and would bring home the whip he used to herd the cattle in the fields to show the family the tool of his travail.

Papa was proud of his twin boys following in his footsteps selling Doubles. They got their own freight bikes when they turned fifteen years old in 1952 and were strong enough to control the bikes with the weight of the Doubles cargo.

Through unquestioning obedience, the twins followed their father's dream and never opposed their role model, because village life and influence had nothing better to offer them. Since formal education was not an option in their future, their lives could not have been self-determined. Among the villagers, their father had earned the reputation of being a successful entrepreneur, so to aspire to that status was a goal worth pursuing.

Papa celebrated this milestone with the first commercial sign for Doubles. The sign was painted on the advertising plate attached to the middle bars of the freight bike. The red-lettered sign on a yellow background proudly proclaimed:

E. DEEN & SONS
SPECIAL HOT CHANA & BARA
SANDWICHES OR DOUBLES

MamooDeen and Rasulan (sitting), Cabil (left), Habil (right)

Taking over from his father in the Princes Town Square, Habil became very popular and attracted all the Doubles customers. His uncle/competitor Choate would have to wait until Habil was sold out before he could sell his Ali's Doubles.

Needless to say, this situation created much resentment in Choate. He became so aggressive in competing with Habil that they ended up in a physical fight that landed them in police custody. Dolo, one of my mother's brothers-in-law, stood bail for Habil's release.

The Expansion to San Juan and Port of Spain

Razack Ali, owner of Amber Records Store in San Juan (pronounced "sah-wah"), traveled the country to buy goats for his meat business. Whenever he was in Princes Town, he would eat Deen's Doubles from Papa, and later they became friends. Being a sharp businessman, Razack Ali saw the novelty and potential of Papa's unique operation and encouraged him to expand his business to San Juan in the north of Trinidad—five miles east of the capital Port of Spain and about fifty miles from Princes Town. Papa found this idea excitingly consistent with his dream of selling Deen's Doubles all across the land.

His determination to chart his own destiny demonstrated a rebellious spirit ready to pull up stakes and move on when things did not work out—a spirit that sustained a northern push to San Juan and the capital city of Port of Spain. The northern frontier promised both opportunity and freedom from Choate's hostile competition in Princes Town. However, he acknowledged that it would be a harsh life in which he would have to depend for his survival on his own wits and labor.

The pride and belief he had in his product gave him the confidence to tackle the challenge of the big city. He was not worried that the city folks did not know his product. He was willing to teach them to like it, one customer at a time. His advertising was by word of the mouths that had tasted his delicious Doubles. What motivated him most to enter unknown territories was his vision of creating a greater demand for Doubles, and he saw an untapped market with no family competition as the ideal opportunity to attain that goal.

Dood's maternal aunt, Imoon Khan, who lived in San Juan, had a house for rent in Petit Bourg on the Eastern Main Road near Jerningham Street. There is still no house number to identify the property except the light pole number LP161. The exact location is the second lot east of Jerningham Street on the northern side of the Eastern Main Road. (The first and second lots east of Jerningham Street are now one business property).

The one-story structure was originally built as a commercial property with two sets of large, swinging, wooden front shop doors. The doors were locked from the inside by heavy wooden bars resting on metal hooks. The building was divided into two apartments, one occupied by relatives of the owner, and the other, on the eastern side, rented by my father for thirty dollars a month. The apartment had three interconnecting rooms and a small area used as a kitchen. There was no privacy because there were no hallways. Access to the front or back of the house was through the rooms. There was no pipe-borne water to the house. Water was brought by buckets and pails from Jerningham Street via a shortcut through the *mitagua* (dry river) at the back of the property. To us running water meant the water we ran with in buckets.

My father built his second Doubles Kitchen in the backyard. It was a wooden shed made from the better pieces of the wooden slabs he used for firewood. The flat roof was made of discarded rusty, corrugated galvanized metal. The structure was built over a dirt floor. Stoves for cooking the Doubles were the same as the Fairfield wood-burning firesides, which were like daily bonfires but without the marshmallows. His expansion plan to San Juan in the north meant taking Cabil along with him and leaving Habil with my mother and the rest of the children.

He introduced his Deen's Doubles in the Croisée (pronounced "kway-say") in San Juan in 1953. His first location was in front of the Bata shoe store on Saddle Road and Second Street. He knew the manager, Raj Ali, from the Princes Town Bata shoe store, who was transferred to San Juan. Raj allowed him to sell his Doubles in front of the store.

On the other side of Second Street was a coconut vendor named Joe Mohammed, who parked his donkey cart full of green coconuts sold for their plentiful "coconut water"—juice—and jelly. Coconut water was and still is a natural complement to the spicy-hot Doubles. Joe Mohammed, who always wore khaki short-sleeved shirts and khaki short pants, was the brother of the famous politician Kamaludin Mohammed. He cut open the coconuts for his customers with a cutlass: he held the coconut in his left hand and trimmed the end to create a small hole from which the customer would drink. His dexterity with the cutlass was a sight to behold. When the customer finished drinking the coconut water, Joe would split open the coconut with precision and cut off a piece of the coconut's skin in the shape of a spoon for the customer to scrape out the delicious jelly. The combination of the Deen's Doubles, coconut water, and coconut jelly for dessert was indeed a delicious, substantial, and complete vegan meal for the man on the go.

My father continued to sell his Doubles in front of the Bata store for some time, until too many street vendors cluttered the entrance to the shoe store and they were all removed by the authorities. He moved across the street to be even closer to Joe, the coconut vendor, where the Chinese Mary's hardware store was located. This street-side location remained the de facto Deen's Doubles location until the late 1980s.

Cabil was given his own freight bike and Doubles Box to sell Deen's Doubles at Johnson's Commercial School in San Juan and at the Ritz cinema on the Eastern Main Road. The benefit of being a mobile street vendor is that you can go to your customers instead of waiting for them to come to you at a fixed building location.

On Sunday mornings, Papa and Cabil would park their Doubles bikes at the southern entrance of the San Juan market. The market was most crowded on early Sunday mornings, when people bought fresh produce and groceries for their special lunch of the week. By noon on Sundays, Papa and Cabil would complete their sales in the San Juan market and head for Fairfield, using four taxis to get there. Because of his generous nature, it was customary for Papa to stop the taxi he was traveling in and buy drinks for all the passengers and the driver. Then they would spend Sunday evenings with us in Fairfield and return to San Juan on Mondays to begin the next week of work. The weekend homecomings were always exciting for the whole family, as Papa and Cabil would always bring goodies for the children and other gifts for the family.

In the early 1950s, the roads and transportation facilities made this journey a major event. Ma would relate that when she left the pristine, pollution-free countryside of Fairfield and passed the oil refinery in Point a Pierre on her way to San Juan, the pungent scent that the polluting refinery produced would make her nauseous and induce bouts of travel sickness.

As the business grew in San Juan, they needed more help. Subrattan was not really enjoying Ecclesville with her new baby, and Dood was still not fully employed. Our father had the ever-so-reliable solution for his unemployed son-in-law: he brought the young family to live with him and Cabil in San Juan and gave Dood a Doubles freight bike to sell Deen's Doubles. Customers called him "Deen" because they thought he was one of MamooDeen's sons.

The other apartment in the divided house became vacant, and Dood and Subrattan occupied it. Subrattan had grown up in the Doubles business in Fairfield, so she was familiar with the work routine. Soon they were operating independent of our father and Cabil but still selling their Doubles under the Deen's Doubles brand name. They were also using the Doubles Kitchen jointly.

Dood sold his Doubles at Osmond High School in San Juan, Cabil took over our father's sales location in the Croisée, and Papa rode his Doubles freight bike to Port of Spain to introduce Doubles to the big city. As in Rio Claro, he again found a rum shop in front of which he sold his

Doubles to intoxicated customers who needed some *cutters*—hors d'oeuvres—as they imbibed their alcoholic beverages. The rum shop was located at the corner of Henry Street and South Quay, Port of Spain. He would sell his Doubles in this location from Tuesday through Saturday and return to the San Juan market on Sunday mornings.

After a few years of selling Deen's Doubles in the San Juan area, Dood and Subrattan quit the business and returned to Ecclesville, Rio Claro, to be near Dood's parents and their agricultural pursuit. Subrattan later became the postmistress for Ecclesville and a coffee and cacao buying agent for Gordon Grant Ltd. She and Dood built a coffee and cacao drying plant on their premises, and Dood transported truckloads of these beans to Gordon Grant Ltd. in Port of Spain for export to international markets.

Chapter 8: The Deaths of the Twins

Habil

Around July 21, 1956, Habil became very ill with a high fever, ague, and bloodshot eyes. Ma took him in desperation to San Juan, where she felt secure with Papa, Cabil, Subrattan, and Dood. Instead of rushing him to the hospital, Papa and Ma took him to a Hindu priest/*obeaman* (shaman) in Aranjuez, San Juan, to be *jarayed*—to get spiritual healing. When that attempt failed and they finally rushed him to the Port of Spain General Hospital, it was too late. He passed away soon after arrival at the hospital on Thursday, July 26, 1956. The official cause of death was the Asian flu.

Chaos and grief ensued. Papa and Ma, with the others from San Juan, returned to Fairfield to break the news to the rest of us waiting eagerly to hear that Habil would be OK. If only we had cell phones then! Subrattan was the first to come out of the taxi. She headed toward us on the front porch. Shaking her head and motioning with her hand, she said Habil was gone! Shock, disbelief, and numbness pervaded the entire household, and soon relatives and neighbors started arriving. Papa showed strength and leadership, but Ma was lost in another world.

Papa went to Amour's Funeral Home in Princes Town and obtained a hearse to go to Port of Spain General Hospital to retrieve Habil's body. The death of an able-bodied nineteen-year-old was traumatic even for the driver of the hearse. He was a very superstitious man; he asked what Habil's favorite drink was and poured whiskey and CC-Mel around the hearse before starting the fifty-five-mile journey from Port of Spain to Fairfield.

Habil's body arrived in an ice box that was placed in the living room for the wake. Villagers constructed a large tent in front of the house. The structural pieces of the tent were made from freshly cut bamboo, and a tarpaulin covered the structure. Our grief was temporarily diverted by the large crowd of people who came to attend the wake and to express their disbelief and condolences. Cabil stayed near the ice box, where it seemed that half of him lay. Ma looked as if she was melting away like the ice that was preserving Habil's body. Prayers were offered, and Muslim *qasidas* (hymns) were sung. Even Boyie, from the cricket-bat incident, was singing in sorrow.

The day of the funeral the crowd was the largest the village had ever seen for a funeral because the identical twins, the Deens' princes of Princes Town, were also the pride of the village, too precious to lose.

Only adult male relatives were allowed to bathe the body and prepare it for the funeral, according to Muslim rites. They placed the body in a purple-satin-lined coffin in the tent for viewing. I recall looking down at the open coffin from the front porch, unable to comprehend the loss of my Big Bhayia.

After the religious rituals were performed, but before Habil's body was taken away, Cabil stood beside the coffin where his twin brother lay and started to sing. Where he got the courage and emotional strength to sing at the saddest moment in our family's life, I will never know. He sang from the depths of his tormented heart the most appropriate song: "O Dhoor ke musafir" ("O Traveler to a Far Place"). Most of the mourners understood the Hindi/Urdu lyrics of the song and its relevance to the surviving twin brother. Everyone was weeping loudly and uncontrollably. The song would become our family's dirge.

The lyrics of the song and its English translation are as follows:

> Song: "O Dhoor ke musafir"
> Movie: *Uran Khatola.* Year: 1955
> Singer: Mohammed Rafi. Musician: Naushad
> Lyrics: Shakeel Badayuni

> *Chale aaj tum jahaan se, huyee zindagee paraayee*
> You leave this world today, my life is not mine anymore
> *Tumhen mil gayaa tikaanaa, humein maut bhee na ayee*
> You found your niche, I didn't even find death
> *O dhoor ke musafir, hum ko bhi saath le le re*
> O traveler to a far place, take me along
> *Hum ko bhi saath le le, hum rahe gaye akele*

Take me along, I am left alone
O dhoor ke musafir, hum ko bhi saath le le re
O traveler to a far place, take me along
Hum ko bhi saath le le, hum rahe gaye akele
Take me along, I am left alone
Thoone wo de diyaa gum, bemauth mar gaye hum
You gave me such grief, I died without dying
Dil ut gayaa jahaan se, le chal humein yahaan se, le chal humein yahaan se
My heart wants none of this world, take me away from here, take me away from here
Kis kaam ki ye duniyaa jo zindagee se khele re
I want nothing of this world, the world that plays with your life
Hum ko bhi saath le le, hum rahe gaye akele
Take me along, I am left all alone
Sooni hai dil ki raahein, khaamosh hain nigaahein
Deserted are the paths of my heart, vacant is my sight
Naakaam hasraton kaa utane ko hai janaazaa, utane ko hai janaazaa
Now is the funeral of my unfulfilled dreams
Chaaron tharaf lage hain, barabaadiyon ke mele re
Devastation all around me
Hum ko bhi saath le le, hum rahe gaye akele
Take me along, I am left all alone
O dhoor ke musafir, hum ko bhi saath le le re
O traveler to a far place, take me along
Hum ko bhi saath le le, hum rahe gaye akele
Take me along, I am left all alone.
(Translated by Saeed@GHI Forums)

One does not have to understand the language of this song to feel the emotions expressed by the immortal voice of Mohammed Rafi when he sang this poignantly sad song, which you can listen to on YouTube. An example of the power of the sound of music is that whenever I play the melody of this song on my harmonium, I can recreate the emotional experience of the funeral as if it happened only yesterday.

According to Muslim custom, women and children do not attend the final rites of interment at the cemetery. When the hearse was departing from in front of our house, Ma's voice, wailing a long and pitiful cry of grief and pain, calling out to Habil, her firstborn, to come back to her, reverberated through the hearts of everyone present and surely throughout the whole village as well. Her cry will remain indelibly etched in my memory for the rest of my earthly existence.

The male-only funeral procession made its way, mainly by foot, to Navet Cemetery, near the town center of Princes Town, about one and a half miles away. There, a Muslim grave had been dug by male friends and relatives, and our Big Bhayia was laid to rest in an unmarked grave according to Muslim custom.

The color purple from the satin lining of the coffin became the color of death to our family, who to this day avoid anything purple.

Ma was on an emotional rollercoaster. She would hold Habil's clothes and try to recapture the scent of her firstborn. She would wake up nights from dreaming about him and call his name out loud as if he were there. I recall her saying, "Habil, are you there? Please say something, boy. Speak to me." Needless to say, her cries awakened the entire household to another episode of grief. She became more and more isolated from us, and our sisters Hamidan and Sharm stepped up to assume more domestic responsibilities.

Cabil tried to fill the void that Habil left in the family and in the Doubles business in Princes Town by moving back home from San Juan. He assumed the dual roles of the twins, and the two personalities would merge into one to provide consolation to the grieving family, relatives, and friends, and even to Habil's girlfriend, who also sought solace from him. His role in comforting us was not only to represent Habil but to stand in for Papa as well, who was left to man the San Juan location with Dood and Subrattan.

Cabil would wear Habil's hat and clothes and imitate his mannerisms in an attempt to distract Ma and the other siblings from the painful emptiness that Habil left. He performed these antics while he himself was quietly pining for the loss of the other half of his existence. He was seen on many occasions singing to his reflection in the mirror and imagining it to be his identical twin brother.

One evening after work, Cabil sat on the floor to play his dholak and sing for the first time after Habil's death. Habil's void was also felt musically, since there was no one to play the harmonium. As if by some divine intervention, I opened the harmonium and started to play it to accompany Cabil as he played his dholak and sang. The first song I played was "Manadole" from the Indian movie *Nagin*. Some of our cousins rushed over to verify that the music they were hearing was real. The harmonium had temporarily resurrected Habil in our home. This would be the start of my love affair with the harmonium, which would grow stronger as the memories grew older.

Early in November of each year, Christians celebrate *latoutsen* (from French La Toussaint, La Tout Saint—All Saints), and the following night is All Souls, when graves were cleaned and those with tombstones and other grave markers were painted. Candles were lit on the graves of the dearly departed. Christianity and Islam merged on that November night in 1956 when, for the love of his brother, Cabil and his friends cleaned up Habil's grave site and lit so many candles on it that it became the brightest one of all. As the candles slowly burned, I sat with Cabil, Palmers, and other friends and relatives around the grave, singing Habil's favorite songs.

Cabil

As the months passed and we were just becoming used to Habil's absence, Cabil became ill, in late September 1957, and was admitted to the San Fernando General Hospital. He was discharged and readmitted with high fever. On Wednesday, October 2, 1957, at the age of twenty, shockingly, Cabil passed away.

We tried feebly to console ourselves with the belief that death to Cabil was his freedom from his tormented life after the loss of Habil, his twin soul mate, and that they were better off together.

The gravity of this second loss so soon, when our tears for Habil were still not yet dried, was indescribably numbing to my already devastated family and the community.

Cabil's death was a tragedy that voraciously devoured the rest of our already frazzled emotions. We were like a family of walking zombies and had to rely on relatives and friends to take control of the situation because Ma became a total nervous wreck, going in and out of a state of semiconsciousness. Papa, who was the tower of emotional and physical strength in the family, became just a shadow of the man—beaten and humbled in speechless grief.

Cabil's funeral to me was more déjà vu than real as the details became blurred. The only vivid memory I have of it is jumping barefoot into a car driven by Raj, a family friend from Curepe, and witnessing the burial of my Lil Bhaiya in a grave next to the grave of my Big Bhaiya. Side-by-side these twin princes of Princes Town came into our lives, and side-by-side they departed. The lives of these inseparable twin brothers ended the way they began: together.

Without the twins, Ma ceased to exist. Her only desire was to be buried next to her firstborn twins, where her unrealized hopes and unfulfilled dreams of a better life were now interred. For her, death was a luxury she would have welcomed.

In her bleak life, the twins had been like two comets that temporarily brightened her dark firmament with broken promises. Their fleeting presence may be a small part of God's grand design, but it remains a monumental tragedy to me, my siblings, and my parents. Habil and Cabil were supposed to be Ma's future sanctuary, where her unforgiving life would be forgotten. But fate had its own hidden agenda.

We had entered a twilight zone where nightmare commingled with reality. Our hearts were broken as our lives fell apart in front of our unbelieving eyes.

As the next few days passed by in silence and prayers, Subrattan, the child bride and now the oldest sibling at nineteen years of age, took charge. She got MunnaBoy, a neighbor with a truck, and with help packed up the remains of our shattered lives; and the family headed for San Juan, where Subrattan, Dood, and Papa were already living. Subrattan had decided that she was not returning to San Juan without the rest of the family. We simply abandoned our homestead in search of sanity.

In the ruthless competition that Choate had created with MamooDeen and his twin sons, Habil and Cabil, for the Princes Town Doubles location, Choate finally won by default. His Ali's Doubles would now enjoy a monopoly in Princes Town and lead to the false claims about the historical origin of Doubles.

Chapter 9: The Family Relocation to San Juan

In our family's move to the north, we were trading despair for a future we could not see. In the geography of our lives, we had seldom been out of sight of a fertile sugarcane plantation, so the urban area of San Juan seemed like an unnatural and sterile environment. The wide-open spaces between the houses in Fairfield were now a luxury lost. The "house" in Petit Bourg, San Juan, was located in close proximity between two other houses, one owned by the principal of a private secondary school and the other by a principal of a commercial school. We felt our private space was invaded. Here, an illiterate Indian family was surrounded by middle-class Afro-Trinidadians who spoke proper English and wore neckties. Mr. Wilson, on the western side, owned the private San Juan Secondary School at Calvary Hill on Real Street, San Juan. Mr. Johnson, on the eastern side, owned the private Johnson's Commercial School in San Juan.

Coming from the predominantly Indian village of Fairfield, where my family had entrepreneurial status, to the diverse town of Petit Bourg in San Juan was socially traumatizing. I lost my racial innocence, quickly learning that I was a "coolie," and was rudely awakened to class consciousness. To be surrounded by urban people who saw us as rural coolies who spoke "broken English" and were involved in an unknown trade was my first awareness of how it feels to be in a lower caste in India.

The immediate benefit of living anonymously in this new location, however, was that in this big empathy void to which we were transplanted, no one knew us or understood the grief we carried as invisible backpacks. We were a wounded family, weary of calamity. Among strangers, we were spared the genuine but depressing sympathies that the Fairfield community would have been expressing to us.

Papa relied on his Doubles business for grief therapy. His courage to believe that despite these major setbacks—the loss of the twins and with them his dream of the prosperity to which they would have contributed; his homestead; the Princes Town sales location, the birthplace of his creation; and the comfort zone for his family in Fairfield—he still could have control over his destiny was an act of persistent optimism that only the best of his human spirit could have invoked and what President Obama has described as "the audacity of hope." It was Papa's audacity still to dream and to find hope inside of ruin that gave our fragmented family the resilience to carry on. It was a critical teachable moment for him to show us how to handle adversity. The gods of encouragement, witnessing his boldness, must have looked on approvingly.

Our mother, however, suffered the most with a nervous breakdown. Her heart was broken with the loss of Habil, but with Cabil's demise so soon afterward, her spirit was now broken. Subrattan and Sharm were our heroes, rising to the challenge of filling the void that our sick mother had created.

They helped us tremendously in moving on as a family unit while our mother slowly healed.

The word "doubles" seems to hold a special significance in our family: the Doubles food business, the double wedding ceremonies of my parents and my mother's brother and father's sister, the double births, and the double deaths of the twins.

Hamidan

Between the twins' deaths, Ma attended a relative's wedding in San Antoine Road near our house and met my sister Hamidan's future husband and his mother. She arranged for a "viewing ceremony," when Waheed Mohammed was introduced to seventeen-year-old Hamidan. Since the family was still in mourning for Habil, no grand wedding could be planned. They were married in a civil ceremony on Friday, September 14, 1957, and a Muslim ceremony on Sunday, September 16, 1957. Hamidan moved in with her in-laws, who were landowners and involved in agriculture in a place called Ants Nest, Tableland.

Her move to Tableland isolated her from the rest of us in San Juan, which was about sixty miles away. Telephone communication was not an option. Public transportation required ten taxis and an entire day for the round trip. As a result, our interaction with her was at a minimum, and she became virtually incommunicado.

The remote country areas that isolated Subrattan and Hamidan from our parents and us siblings emboldened their husbands in the domestic abuse they inflicted on our sisters. In such a culture, the dominant male felt entitled to beat his wife if he so desired because she was his legal property.

Our strong sibling bonds motivated Shamal to take his bicycle on the train from San Juan to visit Subrattan in Rio Claro, then ride over ten miles to Tableland to see Hamidan. Edool, with three high school friends, rode the entire route from San Juan to Tableland via Rio Claro and back, for a total of over 120 miles on dangerous roads, to see our sisters. From time to time, Papa would hire a taxi for a day, and we would all go visit them in the country. As communication technology progressed over the years from gramophone to smartphone, the primitive constraints to interaction were eliminated, making it easier to communicate with Ants Nest from Canada and the United States than it was between San Juan and Tableland fifty years ago.

Hamidan and Waheed could not survive on Waheed's income from picking coffee for fifty cents per day, so they moved to the main road in Tableland, rented Waheed's uncle's house, and started to produce and sell Doubles. Papa gave them a freight bike, a Doubles Box, and other equipment to get started, and taught them the secrets of his trade. The front of the Doubles Box advertised the name Deen's Doubles. Waheed's sales route was from Tableland to Princes Town, a distance of approximately ten miles. After three months there, they moved into our abandoned house in Fairfield to be less than two miles from Princes Town.

Choate and his family did not welcome the new challenge to their monopoly. Waheed was a new face in the business and had no customers. He begged them to give him a break by producing a little less quantity of Doubles so that after they finished their sales, he, Waheed, could get a chance to sell his Doubles. Their response was that instead of making less, they were going to make more Doubles and kill any competition. They did not emulate the selfless quality that MamooDeen exemplified.

A few months passed, and Hamidan was ready to deliver her firstborn. She came to our home in San Juan to have her parents and siblings close to her for this important event in her life. But tragedy struck again when a midwife attempting a home delivery could not handle what turned out to be a complicated birth. When they belatedly rushed Hamidan to the Port of Spain General Hospital, the full-term baby boy was stillborn.

Hamidan and Waheed became extremely despondent from the trauma of losing their first baby boy. During the month Hamidan stayed with us in San Juan to recover, Waheed was unable to produce any Doubles without her help. He quit the business, packed up their belongings, and returned to his parents' home. The Fairfield house was abandoned a second time after the death of another firstborn. Choate and his family were very pleased to regain their Doubles monopoly status in Princes Town.

The Fairfield house remained unoccupied until it was sold in late 1958 for two thousand dollars. After a short time living there, the new owner murdered his wife in a domestic dispute, and the house was abandoned a third time.

The villagers, with their strong superstitious beliefs, are convinced that the property is jinxed. The property, which is now only the land, still remains vacant fifty-six years after we first abandoned it. The once Happy Hill is now a sad reminder of premature death, alcoholism, and domestic violence, and a place of shattered hopes and dreams for my family. Whenever I drive pass this landmark of loss, where my navel string is buried, my heart still skips a beat.

Just when Hamidan thought she had escaped her servility in her in-laws' home to start a life of her own with a new baby, a new business, and living in her father's abandoned house free of charge, fate would have it that she had to return to her in-laws to live in an unhappy extended-family relationship for another five years. Like my mother and other sister, Subrattan, she had to endure domestic violence from her dominant husband and verbal abuse from her parents-in-law. A self-determined life was not an option.

Christianity to the Rescue

We were unaware of any support system to help a grieving mother and her family in this strange new town we had moved to. Then one day, Mrs. Wahid, a Christian Indian lady who lived at the northern end of Jerningham Street, was walking past our house and saw my mother sitting in a hammock, looking out at the street from the emptiness of her funereal world. She walked up to Ma and introduced herself. Mrs. Wahid was truly an angel sent by God to help Ma.

On an almost-daily basis, Mrs. Wahid would visit Ma in her depressed state of mind to counsel, comfort, and pray with her and Sharm. Mrs. Wahid gave Ma a copy of the Holy Bible, which Sharm read to her daily. Sharm's spiritual journey started from meeting Mrs. Wahid and from these readings.

Mrs. Wahid encouraged Ma to go to Mount Saint Benedict and seek help from the many priests who performed counseling services there. Ma took her advice and started to visit the priests, who helped her tremendously in dealing with her unbearable grief. The compelling image of this

Muslim Indian woman wearing her *orhni* in a Catholic monastery showed how desperate Ma was to find peace and embrace life again. Her spirituality had transcended religion.

What was powerfully admirable was that the priests helped her even though she was not a Catholic. Ma continued to make weekly pilgrimages to Mount Saint Benedict, where she would spend most of the day just feeling safe in the sanctity of this spiritually charged refuge.

Hollis (Sabil) Adam Joseph

Hollis. 1959

Papa's love child, Hollis (Sabil), grew up with his mother and visited us from time to time. He was close to his paternal aunts, Rosidan and Kasidan, in Fairfield and San Fernando, respectively. Like our father, whom he closely resembled, Hollis was strongly built, with a fair complexion, and was very handsome.

When he fell in love with Tara, a Hindu girl from Matilda, a village adjoining Fairfield, her father objected on religious grounds. Her father, Mr. Ramjattan Tofan, was a leader of the Hindu community in the area and was well known as the lead organizer of the annual Ram Leela celebrations. Hollis came to San Juan to ask Papa to approach Mr. Tofan for his daughter's hand in marriage. When Papa arrived by taxi at Mr. Tofan's home, he was promptly denied entry and told harshly that no "*madinga*" (a derogatory name for Muslims) was allowed to join the Tofan family. This was despite the fact that Hollis grew up with his mother as a Christian. Hollis and Tara's elopement shortly afterward made any religious objection a nonissue. They were married on December 3, 1959, and became the proud parents of three children: a girl, Jenny, and two sons, Lennard and Junior.

After working several years as a bus conductor, Hollis became interested in the Doubles business, and Papa, without hesitation, taught him the trade in 1968. Hollis started selling Doubles under his father's brand name, Deen's Doubles, but spelt the name *Dean*'s Doubles. He lived with his family in a house near our Fairfield homestead location and sold his Dean's Doubles in direct competition with Choate and his family, who could not deny him his father's space in Princes Town.

It was comforting to Papa to have one of his sons return to Princes Town after eleven years to be the flag bearer for Deen's Doubles in the town of its origin. Hollis continued to sell Doubles for the next nineteen years, until his death on July 10, 1987, at the young age of fifty.

A few years before Hollis' death, he and Tara separated. She sold her own brand of Doubles at the Point-a-Pierre "roundabout" location for several years before migrating with her daughter, Jenny, to the United States.

Gandhi Memorial Vedic School

The calamities of the preceding year and a half had taken a toll on my primary-school education at Craignish EC School in Princes Town, where my education was a casualty of my family's misfortune. I had missed my college exhibition examinations, and no one was really concerned. The family's problems were bigger than school examinations.

Sylvia, a daughter of Mr. Maharaj, the shopkeeper from Matilda junction near Fairfield from whom Papa bought his Doubles supplies, was a teacher at Gandhi Memorial Vedic School in Aranjuez, San Juan. The primary school was within walking distance from Petit Bourg. Papa made arrangements with Sylvia to have me and my two younger brothers, Shamal and Edool, admitted to the school.

He understood the social disruption that the move to San Juan was having on our young lives and tried his best to facilitate the transition by sending us to a Hindu school. At that moment he had to make a choice between his religion and a smooth social transition for us. The Islamic school was much farther away and would have incurred traveling expenses to attend. His religion took second place to the economics and convenience of the Hindu school just walking distance from our home. Also, in the village of Fairfield, Hindus and Muslims were, with few exceptions, truly *jahajee bhais*—brothers of the same boat that brought their ancestors from India. Hindus and Muslims generally lived together like extended families, so sending us to a Hindu school was not a novel socio-religious experiment.

His decision to place me in a Hindu school was a blessing in disguise. It initiated my spiritual journey in understanding the unity of God in the diversity of people's religions. Whenever I play *bhajans* on my harmonium in a Hindu Mandir or *qasidas* and hymns among my Muslim and Christian relatives and friends, I am able to transcend religions through the pervasive force of music—which has no religion, race, caste, gender, or boundaries.

Since we now lived in the big town of San Juan, more attention was paid to the way we had to dress to attend school. In Princes Town, I walked about a mile to primary school, barefooted on a hot asphalt road that had no sidewalks. I recall stepping on a lit cigarette butt that had melted the asphalt beneath it and sustaining a burn to the sole of my foot. The hot, melted, sticky asphalt prolonged the discomfort. Having shoes to wear to school in San Juan was a novelty that boosted our self-esteem and confidence.

When I entered Gandhi Memorial Vedic School, I was placed in standard five. The following year I was in the post-primary class. It was in that class that I finally settled down and found my educational bearings. I read my first novel, *Black Beauty*, in that class. It was an 1877 novel by English author Anna Sewell that became one of the best-selling books in history, with over fifty million copies sold. The book taught me about animal welfare and how to treat people with kindness, sympathy, and respect.

Mr. Roland Ramkissoon was the class teacher. He was the most feared teacher of all. His dual-purpose whip was used as a blackboard pointer and for corporal punishment. Once when I was not paying attention in class, he gave me a "tap" on the back of my head that was so forceful, it busted my lips against the desk, causing profuse bleeding. The fearsome one was himself now scared. He attended to my injury and never abused me again. In fact, I became his favorite student and would ride in his car to and from school.

I took my harmonium to school one day and played it with the choir while they sang *bhajans* (hymns). My playing caused such a sensation that my popularity among the teachers and pupils soared. The high point of my harmonium music at school came when I was asked to play it with my school's choir for *Diwali* in a celebration at the Jubilee cinema in Chaguanas. Several groups from other Hindu schools performed songs and dances on the stage. We were a hit because we were the only choir that had an instrumental accompaniment.

Mr. Ramkissoon was transferred to Rio Claro, and a young bright HC (Higher Certificate—the precursor to A levels) graduate named Leslie Kumar Misir was my new teacher. I soon became his favorite student, and he allowed me to sit on a stool at his large desk. It was such a privilege and honor to be seated literally at the top of my class next to the teacher that it increased my self-confidence tremendously.

My brother Shamal began to show entrepreneurial tendencies at an early age. He and Ma would make pink and white coconut sugar cakes, which he would take to school in a biscuit tin for sale at recess. In addition to receiving his education, Shamal was also receiving a small income from the sale of his sugar cakes. It was the start of an admirable life in business that mirrored the transformational thinking of our father.

Badru (left) and Shamal (right) with Papa in 1958

This photo, taken at Chung's Photo Studio in San Fernando the year after we lost the twins, depicts Papa's grievous need to hold on to the memories of Habil and Cabil. He had taken me and Shamal to visit our cousins in San Fernando and to check on the empty house in Fairfield. We were dressed in our new and best clothes and shoes. Our blue short pants were tailor-made by Paramount Tailors in San Juan; our shirts were from the Kay Shirt Store in San Juan; and our canvas shoes, called "gym boots," were bought from Papa's friend Raj at the Bata shoe store in front of which he sold his Doubles. The sight of MamooDeen with two young sons again at his side was like déjà vu and helped to minimize the sadness and the sympathy our relatives and the villagers felt for his personal loss. Shamal and I were like reincarnations of the twins who were giving Papa a second chance to relive the pride he had in raising Habil and Cabil—his two princes of Princes Town.

Our youngest sister, Shamedan, whom we endearingly call Sharm, was not sent to school when we moved to San Juan because she had reached the "ripe old age of thirteen." She was deprived of an education to take care of our inconsolable mother and perform the domestic duties that Ma was no longer able to perform, either because she was too depressed or too busy helping Papa make Doubles. Sharm cooked our meals, prepared our lunch pails, and washed and ironed our school uniforms, among other domestic duties. She made sure that our school uniforms were always clean, stiff, starched, and ironed. Like Ma, she had to wash clothes by hand using a scrub board, commonly called a "juking board," in a tub of soapy water. She ironed our clothes by heating the flatiron over the coal pot.

Our cultural and religious norms from Fairfield were, of course, not shed on arrival in the big town of San Juan; it would take time for us to adapt, and for now the old rules applied. Sharm had to stay home and prepare for a married life of endearing servility, making children, and performing domestic duties, like her mother and two older sisters before her. She dutifully accepted her fate with her trademark cheerful smile and never complained. To me and my two younger brothers (Shamal and Edool), Sharm was our second mother. The four of us developed such a special bond of love among us that our own respective spouses and children cannot fathom the intensity of our sibling relationship. I personally owe Sharm a lifelong debt of gratitude for providing the support system at home that facilitated my early education.

Sharm recalled her embarrassment at being seen by the neighbor's sons, who were curious to see her making *sada roti* (flatbread) on a *tawa* over a wood-burning fireside. The neighbors had already graduated to gas stoves in a proper kitchen. In their eyes, we were rural rubes for whom time had stood still. We had a lot of catching-up to do in this new environment, where our life's circumstances were weighing down on our confidence.

Jamaloo, at fifteen years old, was given his own Doubles freight bike and started selling Deen's Doubles in the same location in San Juan that Cabil had occupied. The loss of his twin brothers seemed to have affected Jamaloo differently. He had unexpectedly become the oldest son, with major responsibilities placed on his young shoulders. He was now required to help Papa sell Doubles. He never complained in assuming this responsibility that was thrust on him, but he became even more of a quiet and aloof brother, as if his grief for the loss of Habil and Cabil manifested in a silent protest against life's turn of events.

The whole family, except for Ma, came down with a bout of chicken pox. Papa was hit exceptionally hard by the illness. He asked Ma to bring him a drink of alcohol to ease the pain, but he could not finish it after the first sip. It was to be his last taste of alcohol. After his recovery he quit drinking alcohol "cold turkey" and shortly afterward also gave up smoking cigarettes. To give up alcohol and tobacco after twenty-five years of addiction showed his strength of character in freeing himself from the abyss of addiction. To have done it without any professional intervention was indeed a resurrection of sanity when his misery became his therapist. His moment of awakening had finally arrived. His ability to transform his life repeatedly demonstrated the determination of a freedom fighter.

Being victims of the ravages of alcoholism and domestic violence motivated Shamal, Edool, and me to focus our young lives in a sober direction.

The Old Road House

Papa started to attend the Real Street Mosque on Fridays, where he met a man named Hakim who had a house for sale on Santa Cruz Old Road, San Juan. The house was situated near the corner of Petit Curacaye Road and Santa Cruz Old Road at Light Pole No. 50. House numbers were never assigned, but some folks were assertive enough to choose their own numbers for their addresses. The house was on the eastern side of the road on a hill facing one of the many mountains of the Northern Range.

After viewing the property with his friend Roodal Nandalal, Papa bought it for $2,700. He used the proceeds of the sale of the abandoned Fairfield house (which he'd sold for $2,000 in 1958) and paid off the $700 balance in installments of $50 per month. Roodal, with his truck, helped us move from Petit Bourg to the house on Santa Cruz Old Road.

The walls of this house were constructed from *tapia,* which is made from a mixture of mud and straw placed between supporting sticks and plastered smoothly with cement. The roof was corrugated galvanized metal, the floor wooden. The house sat on short concrete pillars that allowed only a little more than crawl space underneath. It had four and a half rooms and a small front porch. There was no pipe-borne water or indoor plumbing. Water was collected from the rain in steel barrels and replenished by bucket from the nearby public standpipe.

Half of the house—two and a half rooms—was rented to two Afro-Trini families by the previous owner. The tenants, Redman, Dorothy, and their three children, lived in the back room, and Patsy with her father and grandmother lived in the one-and-a-half-room space. The tenants were given notice to vacate, which they did shortly afterward, and for the first time since leaving Fairfield, we had an entire house to ourselves. It is interesting to note that with each of the three houses we lived in, our family had to start off occupying half the house.

The third Doubles Kitchen was built on the northeastern corner of the lot, adjoining the house. The neighbor on the northern side objected to the unsightly structure made of uneven slabs of wood for walls and of used, rusty sheets of corrugated galvanized metal, from the second Doubles Kitchen in Petit Bourg, on the roof. It was simply a dilapidated shed that did not add to the value of the property.

Shamal, Edool, and I now had to commute by bus to attend school. The bus would let us off in the Croisée, and we would walk the rest of the way to the Gandhi Memorial Vedic School in Aranjuez. The bus fare to and from the Croisée for the three of us totaled twenty-four cents. We were given a quarter, so we rotated the one-cent change among the three of us. When we felt adventurous, we would spend the bus fare and walk home from school, a distance of about three miles.

Alick and Sharm

The next-door neighbors on the south side of our house were Mr. Ali and his wife, Kala. Mr. Ali was a tailor who worked from his front porch. He always had customers and friends hanging around as he sewed their clothes. Among his friends was Alick Paguandas, a tall, handsome young man with a fair complexion. He was a customs clerk who wore a necktie to work. The colonial necktie was the inherited symbol of success that distinguished the wearer from the common folk and allowed him to mimic the colonists' power over the colonized.

Alick started to pay attention to my sister Sharm as she made repeated trips to the public standpipe for buckets of water. The standpipe was in front of Mr. Ali's house, so Alick could not avoid setting eyes on her. There must have been some mutual attraction because Sharm became overly conscientious in her water-carrying chore. Our water barrels were soon as overflowing with water as Sharm was overflowing with emotions for Alick.

They started chatting over the short hibiscus hedge that separated our property from Mr. Ali's. Sharm's conversations with Alick were so engrossing that she was oblivious to her nervous reaction of plucking the leaves off the hibiscus hedge, which denuded that section of the fence. Soon Alick was helping her tote water, and our barrels overflowed rapidly. Our whole family was pleased to welcome him. We were so eager to have a surrogate big brother fill the void of the missing ones: Habil and Cabil.

When the relationship started to get serious, Mr. Ali intervened to save his friend Alick from making a social mistake in joining this "low-class Doubles family." The wife of one of Alick's cousins, a woman of mixed heritage, who lived across the street from us, also volunteered marital advice, discouraging Alick from getting involved with a "low-class coolie family." From the time we relocated to this area until her death, this lady never became close to our family; she made the sign of the cross whenever our gazes intersected.

Luckily, Alick paid no attention to the unsolicited advice he was getting from those prejudiced people. It is said that true love is the untarnished truth that beats in pure hearts that see no hurdles or boundaries in human relationships. As Alick continued to spend more time with us, my two younger brothers and I developed a special relationship with him. He became our friend for life. When a son of our new community genuinely accepted us, we felt we had crossed a milestone in social acceptance. Alick was the knight in shining armor who rescued the poor damsel and brought back smiles to the faces of her family.

In choosing Alick, Sharm became the trailblazer in breaking down the tradition of arranged marriages in our family. The relationship led to their marriage on June 10, 1962, the year Trinidad and Tobago gained its independence. Alick moved in with us in an extended-family arrangement. This was the first time that one of our sisters got married and did not have to live with and be subservient to her parents-in-laws.

They produced two children, Lyra and Larry, and later emigrated to Canada, where Alick worked for the Inco Mining Company in Sudbury, Ontario, until his retirement. Sharm became a much-sought-after wedding dressmaker and fashion designer. She generated her own cash flow from her fashion designing and wedding-dress-making endeavors and from jobs she held at the local hospitals. Unlike my mother and two other sisters in Trinidad, Sharm is the first female in my family to drive an automobile and gain some economic independence from her husband. Lyra and Larry are successful university graduates employed as tax auditors with the Canadian government. Alick, like the miner he became later in Sudbury, discovered a diamond in the rough when he found Sharm, who became his lifelong soul mate.

Chapter 10: The Start of a New Direction

My mother attended my graduation from post-primary school, and my teacher, Mr. Leslie Kumar Misir, pleaded with her to send me to a private secondary school because he had seen that I had the potential for higher education and transformation.

On her return home, Ma told Papa what my teacher had said and begged him to send me to high school. Drawing from her life lessons from her surrogate mother and mentor, Masitan, who chose the educational path for her three sons, James, John, and George, gave her the confidence to persuade Papa to try a new direction for at least one of their sons. She had seen how education had opened doors for Masitan's twins, James and John West, which were closed to her twins, Habil and Cabil. She was willing to take the risk that could make me their white cane to lead them in their blindness of the literate world.

My father initially resisted the idea since his dream was for all his sons to grow up to be Doublesmen. So to educate me was to lose a potential Doublesman and lose control over my destiny. He saw all the able-bodied males around him as potential Doublesmen. So far he had succeeded in creating Doublesmen out of his two brothers-in-law, Asgar and Choate; Rasulan's cousin Aziz; his twin sons, Habil and Cabil; his sons-in-law Dood and Waheed; and later, his sons Jamaloo, Hollis, and Shamaloo and grandsons Balo and Tasmool. His brother, Babwa, was the only male in his family circle who did not join him in the Doubles business, choosing instead to work for a bakery selling bread from a van.

I believe that after losing the twins, Papa, like Ma, was also questioning his family business plans for the remaining sons. One day soon after the discussion with my mother, he pushed his heavy freight bike up the steep Calvary Hill from the Croisée, a distance of about a mile, to see the principal of San Juan Secondary School, located at the top of Real Street. The principal, Mr. Wilson, had been our next-door neighbor when we lived in Petit Bourg and knew Papa well.

This was a critical moment in my father's life. He was, for the first time, thinking that one of his sons would not become a Doublesman, and his dream of creating a Doubles empire with his six sons was reduced to just that—a dream. It took a great deal of courage and foresight on his part to deviate from his vision for my future and allow me to attend high school, a move that would arrest the transgenerational transmission of illiteracy that had dominated our heritage like a genetic disease for which a cure was finally found.

High School: A New Road

Letting me go to high school was a sea change in my formative years; it would give me the freedom to dream my own dreams, to live my own life, and to follow a new road out of the Old Road. The gods of continuity in the Deen's Doubles business that had hovered over my boyhood were now setting me free to chart my own destiny.

I was accepted by Mr. Wilson and placed in Form 2B to start my secondary education. Tuition was TT$18 per term. Tuition for the five years of my secondary school education totaled TT$270. The course load included English, Latin, Spanish, French, mathematics, geography, and Christian scripture. Latin helped me tremendously in learning English, Spanish, and French. I knew then that if I missed this educational opportunity, I would be riding a Doubles freight bike into my future. Like my father in his leap of faith to leave the agrarian lifestyle behind, I was extremely motivated to think outside the Doubles Box.

There was no educational support at home to help me with my homework. I had to figure it out on my own. I cannot imagine the helpless feeling my parents must have endured being unable to help me with my academic homework. They placed their faith in me and my teachers. Mr. Wilson did not disappoint them. He was my role model and helped shape my life in my formative years. The language courses in Latin, English, Spanish, and French, together with geography, piqued my curiosity for other cultures and countries.

I placed first in the final exams in three consecutive terms of my first year and was promoted to form four for the following year, skipping form three. My father was so proud of me that he bought me my first new bicycle from Mr. Cave in San Juan—how relieved I was that my first new bicycle was not a Doubles freight bike! My bike symbolized the different road on which I must ride and not follow any predetermined course set by someone else. My new direction started with not going into my family's business.

My parents were pleased with their investment in my education, and it gave them the confidence to consider higher education also for my two younger brothers. Seeing Shamal's aptitude for business, they sent him to Bally's Commercial School to study accounting and bookkeeping, and Edool was enrolled at Mr. Wilson's San Juan Secondary School during my last year there.

Ma really wanted me to follow a new direction and tried to make sure that I was not distracted by any of the vices that had led Papa astray. So she gave away our harmonium without my knowledge. I felt it was mine since I was the only one in the family who was playing it. Papa had also given up on playing music, as he had given up alcohol and cigarettes. Even though I understood her fear, it was a heart-wrenching experience to lose my harmonium. Its melodious sound would never be heard again within the walls of my parents' home. I felt that this beautiful musical instrument was given a bad rap by my mother only because she associated it with my father's vices. The same instrument accompanying hymns and bhajans in the church or mandir makes the spiritual experience so much more powerful. Most of the greatest Indian singers from India were accompanied by the harmonium in their recordings and live performances. The harmonium certainly helped the Indian diaspora in Trinidad to maintain their ethno-musical roots.

Some twenty years later, in the early 1980s, when Ma visited my home in Miami for the first time and saw my electronic keyboard, she accusingly asked, "You playing again?" For thirty years I would stay away from the harmonium—until I went to India and could not resist buying one. Like never forgetting how to ride a bicycle, playing the harmonium came back to me—just as the memories of the Doubles Kitchen return when I smell the pungent aromas of some spices. The harmonium could be taken away from me, but no one could take me away from the harmonium.

The most important gift I received from my father was a used leather-bound two-volume set of the *Unabridged Webster's Dictionary*. They were the biggest books I had ever laid eyes on. Someone with more need for money than knowledge of the English language had sold it to him in Port of Spain. I do not know how much he paid for it or if he knew what kind of book he had bought. Maybe he was impressed by the size and the leather covers. Maybe the seller explained to him its importance for my high school education, and he trusted the seller's sales pitch.

After his day's sales of Doubles were completed, he placed the dictionaries in the empty chana container in the Doubles Box to bring them home. (Luckily for the leather-bound covers, it was easy to clean the curry stains they sustained from the chana container.) Going from being so suspicious of books that he even burned the twins' comic books, to buying a book for me that contained all the words of the English language, was indeed a major transformation in his thinking. What resonated most was receiving the gift of the English language from my illiterate father, who lived his whole life not knowing how to speak the language properly.

Those two volumes of *Webster's Dictionary*, more than anything else, contributed to my facility with the English language. They were like "double tutors" Papa had hired to give me private lessons in a subject he was unable to teach me. These dictionaries were my constant companions in all the places I lived in my life's journey, from Trinidad to Winnipeg, Morden, and Regina, back to Trinidad, and finally to Miami, where they even survived Hurricane Andrew in 1992. Cleaning the mud of Hurricane Andrew from their leather-bound covers brought back the memories of cleaning the curry stains off them thirty-two years before.

The more I focused on formal education, the more I was able to see the Doubles business from the outside in. I saw how the ignorant and critical public could not understand the incubation phase of a new fledgling industry and viewed it as a man "begging for a living at the side of the road."

Bullying and Shame

Children would mock me and my younger brothers with names such as "DoublesBoys" or "ChanaBoys," especially when we were trying to impress the pretty girls in school. They whispered and giggled and tried to make us feel like people with a disability who are callously ridiculed by ignorant bullies. During one heckling session, I was kicked off my bicycle by a bully named Hector. His attack caused severe lacerations to my arms and knees, requiring the intervention of the principal, Mr. Wilson, who punished the big bully with a few strokes of his belt. On another occasion, a bully with a pair of scissors clipped off the hair curl I wore over my forehead. My hairstyle was my attempt to imitate Sal Mineo, the teen movie star of the 1950's.

The put-downs were painful coming from children, but extremely destructive to my self-esteem and confidence when the belittling came from a teacher who was scolding my youngest brother, Edool, in the same high school. He told him, "Deen, pay attention, or you will end up like your brother selling Doubles on the street." It turned out that while sticks and stones could have broken our bones, those words really hurt us. As Silvan Tomkins (quoted by Donald Nathanson in 1992) said, "The humiliated one feels himself naked, defeated, alienated, lacking in dignity and worth."

In my critical period of development, when I was very self-conscious and sensitive to negative stimuli, the belittling permeated my consciousness; I felt my own dignity as a human being was devalued by others. The experience denied me my right to be proud of my father's creation because it was made a target of ridicule. In the absence of positive social acceptance of my father's business, shame infiltrated my pride during my impressionable years. It would take a long time to exorcise the shame I experienced during this critical developmental period.

It was not unusual for people to make fun of the disabled in an attempt to be funny. Since I had no distinguishing features of which to make fun, children must have thought that my father's business was fair game because of its novelty and uniqueness.

To defend the insensitive behavior of the children who were picking on me as the pastime of "giving fatigue" (teasing) is to accept the abuse as normal and that I am flawed.

Bullying was an attack on my self-respect and dignity. Because I did not have the power to change the bullying situation and stand up for myself, I struggled with it throughout the pursuit of my secondary education. A study published in the August, 2013 edition of *Psychological Science* concludes: "Being bullied is not a harmless rite of passage or an inevitable part of growing up, but throws a long shadow over affected children's lives." Psychologists now advise that the traumatic experiences sensitive children endure from peer ridicule and bullying can last a lifetime and sometimes even lead to suicide. In June 2013, the local press reported that the minister of education, Dr. Tim Gopeesingh, was addressing the issue of bullying in schools. If fifty-three years ago, parents, teachers, and students were sensitized to the psychological effects that bullying can have on its victims, my brothers and I would have been spared the horrible experience.

Despite being made fun of in school, I stayed focused on my academic mission and remained a top student throughout my high school years. The humiliation actually propelled my desire to excel academically and motivated me to be creative in my strategies for survival in a tough environment. It must have been my father's confidence in entering and penetrating markets in new territories with his Doubles that influenced my ability to deal with peer ridicule and bullying. My best friends in high school, who never judged me by my father's work, were the support group that helped to boost my self-esteem and confidence. They were Winston "Lowie" Low Sin, Zamule "Z" Ali, and Najib Ali, who remained my friends for life.

In the 1950s, when my father was introducing Doubles to the non-Indian population in the north, the marketing of Indian foods to the masses was still in its infancy. Haute cuisine did not include curry dishes; roti and dhal were coolie foods. Indians were generally embarrassed to eat their ethnic foods publicly, especially in secular schools and work places. The familiar derogatory refrain from non-Indians that ridiculed Indians and their cuisine was: "Coolie, coolie, come for roti, all de roti done." So, in such an environment, for Papa to launch a new product like Doubles was indeed a bold venture that took *cojones*. My father was so confident in his creation that he was prepared to persuade one customer at a time to try, oftentimes gratis, his delicious snack. He believed in his product and was convinced that hungry humans—Indian or non-Indian—would satiate their hunger with this delicious comfort food.

In this social environment and in my young and impressionable mind, I started to look at the Doubles business as the antithesis of a higher education and upward mobility because children did not go to school to become Doublesmen. My curry culture was far from being mainstreamed, especially in the northern areas of Trinidad. Instead of recognizing the entrepreneurial creativity of my father's efforts, a teacher at Gandhi Memorial Vedic School admitted to me several years later that she felt pity for me and my two younger brothers in school because our father and brother sold Doubles for a living.

One Saturday morning I went by taxi to replenish the supply of Doubles for my brother, Jamaloo, in the Croisée in San Juan. Returning with an empty container placed inside a curry-stained flour bag, I was on the bridge over the San Juan River on Real Street awaiting a taxi when I saw a classmate approaching from a distance. In a reflex action, I threw the container in the river in what was, as I realized in retrospect, a physical gesture of trying to avoid the shame I was experiencing as a son of the Doublesman. I felt immense continuous pressure carrying the burden of this shame, which felt worse than poverty itself. It led to a series of emotions like humiliation, embarrassment, feelings of low self-esteem, belittlement, and stigmatization.

Selling Doubles somehow seemed to be advertising our poverty, which made me feel even more insecure. It is said that the curse of poverty is that it sounds untrue to people who have not experienced it. I began to feel jealous of all those who were not poor. I was too young to understand that poverty could be spiritually transformative. Writing now about my poverty is to discover that poverty had already written my destiny.

As a result of the early negative perception of Doubles, it mainly appealed to disadvantaged schoolchildren, poor people, and drunkards with loose change in their pockets. This fact is substantiated by my father and brothers selling Deen's Doubles at or near the entrances of schools and rum shops in Princes Town, Rio Claro, San Juan and Port of Spain. My brothers and a brother-in-law sold Deen's Doubles near the entrances of Osmond High School and El Socorro Islamic elementary school at lunchtime. Our cousins in San Fernando sold Ali's Doubles at the Naparima College and were also located in front of a rum shop on High Street.

But the strategy of selling Doubles to schoolchildren developed a captive clientele who would grow up to be repeat customers for life. Schoolchildren were the best ambassadors for Doubles. As adults they recall with nostalgia eating a delicious Doubles when they were poor, hungry students.

This rudimentary sales strategy was no different from the sophisticated marketing strategies used today by multinational corporations such as McDonald's, Burger King, and Wendy's in promoting their fast foods to children.

Customers who did not belong to these lower-class target groups would approach the Doubles Box timidly, make a quick purchase, and disappear to eat them at home or elsewhere. They could not be seen eating Doubles on the street. Those who were brave or hungry enough would stand and eat with such rapidity that they made the product the fastest fast food in the land. I am inclined to believe that the quick dexterity of wrapping Doubles originated from attempting to minimize the embarrassment of this higher class of customers who were apprehensively patronizing the Doublesman.

The stigma of the perception that street foods are unsanitary prevails to this day. In an article in the *Trinidad Express* on January 16, 2011, titled "Carnival and Food Safety," a picture of Doubles being sold was the only image of a street food shown, even though the article was about all street foods. It must be the popularity of Doubles that puts it in the spotlight and makes it an easy target for some local journalists to make unsubstantiated claims about Doubles being unsanitary. If Doubles were killing people, as the article inferred, most of the population of Trinidad would have been wiped out in the seventy-seven years that they have been eating Doubles.

Some folks are not able to tolerate pulse foods, curry and other spices, or the hot sauces served in Doubles. Also, when customers don't wash their hands, they may contaminate the Doubles, making their gastronomic discomfort self-induced. If some street vendors are not adhering to strict sanitary rules, it may also reflect on the public health safety authority's lax enforcement of the rules.

Doubles vendors need to form an organization that will represent and defend the industry from such libelous claims. The beef industry in the United States got the great Oprah Winfrey, who was threatened with a major lawsuit, to retract and apologize for the negative statements she made against beef on her television program addressing the topic of mad-cow disease.

In July 2010, I was making an airline reservation on the phone in Miami, Florida. The agent was a Trinidadian expatriate living in the United States. During our conversation she mentioned that she was from San Juan, Trinidad, so I asked her if she had known about Deen's Doubles in San Juan. She said no and added that her parents did not allow her and her siblings to eat street foods like Doubles. I was surprised that she did not make the connection between my last name, Deen, on the reservation and the Deen's Doubles we were talking about. I aborted the topic of Doubles but not without the persistent gnawing feeling of rejection of my father's creation, which is so easily criticized by ignorant people with ulterior motives. For each of the remaining folks who persist in denigrating Doubles, there are thousands who are enjoying the delicacy.

I empathize with the street vendors of the world who are simply making a living feeding their customers, not trying to poison them. I am impressed with the exciting taste experiences I continue to have in my international travels and identify with Anthony Bordain, the popular TV food show host of *No Reservations*, who takes great pleasure in discovering, tasting, and reporting on the street foods of the world.

Starting to Turn Away from Doubles

I started to look at the Doubles business like my father had looked at the agrarian lifestyle that he abandoned creatively. Although the Doubles business paid the bills and fed our family, we had by no means conquered necessity. It took great courage to live ordinary lives of involuntary simplicity. I hated being poor.

Doubles was an unknown street food to the Santa Cruz Old Road community. People could not understand what motivated my brother Jamaloo and my father to choose such a hard way to make a living. They pedaled their heavy freight bikes on the hilly roads to and from the Croisée in San Juan, and in my father's case, also in the busy traffic on the Eastern Main Road to and from Port of Spain, a ten-mile return trip. They had to dismount their freight bikes and push them up the hilly roads, and they rested while coasting downhill. Their commitment to the business blinded them to exploring any other alternative work as they remained focused and motivated in perfecting and promoting Deen's Doubles. Their daily challenge was to have the demand for Deen's Doubles equal to its supply. When a successful day's sales were accomplished, the whole family felt motivated to perform the chores for the next day's sales.

The Doubles business was hard work that required the physical effort of the entire family. The long hours would start at 3 a.m. during the week and midnight on Saturday nights to catch the early morning shoppers at the San Juan Market on Sunday mornings. To keep my mother awake in the smoke-filled, hot Doubles Kitchen, my father would sing for her. Heat without smoke was not an option given the wood-burning firesides, so they had to endure the unforgiving smoke in their eyes and lungs to complete the daily supply of Doubles. I felt guilty going to sleep while they worked.

The early morning production and sale soon conditioned customers to make Doubles their breakfast staple. Deen's Doubles were sold for breakfast and lunch and never at night. The afternoons and early evenings were for preparations for the next day's production and sale. My parents' commitment to have the Doubles ready to satisfy the customers' hunger was the motivating force that kept them always busy. Although they were their own bosses, their dedicated determination to satisfy their customers kept them on a schedule of urgency.

Their haste was frustrated one carnival Monday morning called *j'ouvert* (from French *jour ouvert*—opening day) when Jamaloo arrived late after partying the night before. We were preparing from the day before, and our parents had been up since midnight to have Doubles ready for the thousands of revelers and spectators coming from the many fetes to start the carnival. It was the first time I heard my father express how much he missed the twins. He was filled with emotion when he said, "If only Habil and Cabil were here, there would be no delay."

Unlike the other children in this community whose fathers worked outside their homes, our family business brought work into our home. Our homework did not only mean school studies. After school and on weekends, my two younger brothers and I helped by washing the pots and pans, bringing the firewood into the Doubles Kitchen, grinding spices in a hand mill, peeling onions and garlic, and cutting the paper wraps. My innovative father figured out that by using a "grass knife"—a hand-held sickle with a wooden handle and a sharp, serrated semicircular edge—he could fold the large, flat sheets of Hercules brown paper and easily cut multiple sheets to the required size with straight edges. This was a transfer of knowledge from cutting grass for the animals to cutting paper for Doubles. A paper guillotine was an unknown tool to us at that time. These responsibilities in our formative years certainly molded our characters away from becoming delinquents or victims of other social deviations.

In the Santa Cruz Old Road area where we lived, there were a high percentage of mixed-race people. They were of Afro-Indian, Afro-white, Indo-Spanish, and Spanish origin. African families made up the majority of the people in this area, with the few Indian families in the minority. It was certainly not an Indian village like Fairfield, Princes Town.

The progressive Indian families were mainly Christians. Whenever they heard us speak, they would correct our broken English. Our Fairfield lingua franca clashed with the Santa Cruz dialect, which aspired to imitate the Queen's English. A rapid language adjustment was necessary for my siblings and me to interact with this new "higher class" of people.

Their lifestyle was also different from ours in many ways. Some whose homes I visited had upholstered Morris chairs in living rooms with polished wood floors. Their fathers and adult siblings had jobs outside the home. We basically lived in our parents' business, surrounded by responsibilities that were both domestic and commercial. The other residents listened to American music from their radiograms and held dancing parties regularly. We played Indian music on our own instruments and entertained ourselves. They baked bread, we made roti. They ate pork, which was taboo in our Muslim home. Some had automobiles; we had bicycles. They celebrated all the Christian holidays with great fanfare. To us, Christmas was more like it was in Varanasi, India, where it is not celebrated by the greater Hindu population—it was just another day.

Proselytized Indians were better integrated into the new society that the colonial masters were creating. In their social experiment, the colonists succeeded in imposing their economic and religious powers on the "imported natives" of Trinidad and Tobago. Proselytized Indians achieved upward social mobility by changing their names, religion, diet, attire, music, and language; in short, they had to trade their ethnicity and culture for education and socioeconomic progress. Colonists must have believed that "proselytizing the colonized would legitimize the colonization."

In that evolving new society, the young Deens seemed qualified to fail. To paraphrase Anchee Min, we were like boiled chana seeds with no chance to sprout. It felt like we were being punished for holding on to our ancestral traditions in a society that tried to marginalize the Indian culture.

In my confused state of mind and in need of social acceptance, I started to attend Christian church services with some of my Christian friends and almost got baptized as a Christian. Even though Sharm was already reading Mrs. Wahid's Christian Bible for Ma and was internalizing its teachings, it was love that made her a Catholic. By choosing Alick Paguandas, a Catholic Indian, as the love of her life, she had also chosen her religion.

Being a cultural Muslim rather than a religious Muslim allowed me to explore and understand the essence of the three religions to which I was exposed: Islam, Hinduism, and Christianity. I leaned toward the belief that "all religions have God, but God has no religion." I felt that I should be allowed to choose my own beliefs and make an informed decision about religion, and so I did not impose religion on my own children. I was satisfied in taking the best from these religions and have tried to live by their universal teaching—do unto others as you would have others do unto you.

I recall two of the many humiliating incidents that might have reinforced my desire to turn away from the Doubles business. One was when my father was pedaling his Doubles freight bike on his way home from Port of Spain. He was on the Saddle Road in Central Village near our home. An aspiring teenaged "badjohn" (bandit) aimed his slingshot and fired a two-pointed, U-shaped nail at my father. The young man's aim was accurate; his projectile hit my father's arm, causing pain and profuse bleeding. My father jumped off his bike, parked it on the road, and ran after the young man, who disappeared in the nearby bushes. Papa arrived home with a bloody arm and blood-soaked clothing, angry and vengeful. How frustrating it was to be physically attacked while simply trying to earn an honest living to provide for one's family. The whole family felt my father's physical and psychological pain of being a target for the ignorant.

The other incident was when my father, along with some pedestrians, was sheltering from a heavy rainfall under the eaves of Atwell's Drug Store in the Croisée. In the crowd was an adult badjohn who wanted to entertain the crowd at my father's expense. The badjohn started to push the bike and my father back and forth into the rain to the amusement of the crowd. Papa said he thought of reaching into his Doubles box for the sharp cutlass he carried, but instead meditated on the consequences of such a reaction and although feeling the sting of humiliation, rode off in the rain.

I will never know how many more instances of embarrassing ridicule my father and brothers must have endured in promoting Deen's Doubles. Like other street vendors, they were also subjected to frequent police harassment to keep them off the streets and sidewalks. The freight bikes were extremely functional in circumventing the harassment since they could easily be moved to another location.

Badjohns frequently intimidated and extorted money from them. It is called a "coward tax" when peaceful and timid vendors hand over their hard-earned money to these bullies. Some of these badjohns justified their ill-gained loot by claiming they were protecting the vendors from other bullies. Jamaloo related many instances of having to hand over his hard-earned cash to these bold bandits, but the one that stands out most in my mind is the bandit who urgently demanded cash to buy disposable diapers for his baby! Vendors were so intimidated by these bullies that they would not get the police involved for fear of violent retribution. It is a sad situation that persists even today. The bandits have been emboldened by lack of retaliation from the vendors and the absence of police protection. They now have the power to determine how much income a Doubles vendor deserves— as reported on a blog in a local newspaper about the bandit who told the Doubles vending couple that their sales from Monday to Friday are for the couple and the sales from Saturday and Sunday are for him! My outrage for this injustice numbs my senses.

An experience that remains vivid in my memory was when our house was finally connected to pipe-borne water from the Water and Sewage Authority (WASA) after being on a waiting list for several years. A truckload of about ten men, including their supervisors, came to make the connection. The work took about an hour to complete, after which time the ten men were treated to a sumptuous lunch of curry chicken, dhalpourries, and Scotch whiskey. It was the incentive my father had to give in order to get the water connection. In the prevailing corrupt system, we were made to feel that we had received a huge favor from WASA for performing their job. Paying the badjohns and bribing officials to perform their duties were survival strategies.

My father was a very charitable man. One of his charitable acts had a profound effect on us and the surrounding Christian community in which we lived. Although all religions teach us about serving the poor, it was unusual to invite and actually serve them at one's home. On the first Sunday of each month, Papa would invite beggars from the Croisée for lunch at our home. We all helped in serving the beggars, who would number a dozen or more. After lunch Papa would give them some monetary offerings and clothing. Before they left, they would show their gratitude by offering a prayer according to their respective religious persuasions. The simultaneous unifying sound of their prayers echoed the universal truth of the One source of religions and humanism that resides in the diverse religions of the world.

James West and My First Job

After my graduation from San Juan Secondary School, I applied for a government scholarship to Australia. From my youthful readings, I was fascinated with Australia and New Zealand and fantasized about studying there and discovering the lifestyle of the indigenous Maori Indians of New Zealand. I was very disappointed when I did not even receive an acknowledgment of my application for the scholarship. The awarding of scholarships seemed to be influenced by political patronage, class, and race.

I had also applied to the Public Service Commission for employment and received no response. My mother stepped in again, this time to jump-start my employment. She asked her cousin James West to help me find a job. He had recently returned from Canada as a highly qualified chartered accountant. He took me in to see an official in charge of placements at the Red House, and I was asked to report for work shortly thereafter, in January 1965, at the Treasury, Ministry of Finance, located on Independence Square in Port of Spain. Although he was embraced by the "entrenched elite" group, as Dr. Ken Boodhoo describes this ruling class in his book *The Elusive Eric Williams*, James West was in fact an Indian incognito who spoke fluent Hindi and had no qualms about assisting a Fairfield Indian relative facing racial inequality in the Public Service. I owe James West my sincere gratitude for breaking down the first barrier to my upward social mobility.

My starting salary was TT$110.00 (US$22.92) per month, which was the most money I had ever earned. To have one of MamooDeen's sons not selling Doubles but becoming a necktie-wearing civil servant speaking proper English was a proud moment for the whole family.

Mr. Jean Charles was the comptroller of the Treasury; Mrs. Ng Fan was in charge of personnel; and Mr. Forgenie, Mrs. Roxborough, Mr. Farfan, and Miss Lynette Bellsmythe were supervisors. What was quite conspicuous was the hierarchy of skin pigmentation in the organizational chart of the Treasury, which was a holdover from the colonial era.

Skin pigmentation was a function of status and social class in society—the lighter the skin complexion, the higher the status and social class. The Treasury's hierarchy reflected Trinidad's social dynamics: the colonial whites were on top, followed by French Creoles, Chinese, mulattoes, people of mixed races, Africans, Christian Indians, and finally Hindu and Muslim Indians. In addition to the racial differences, there were the intragroup color dynamics of preferential treatment for lighter-complexioned individuals. The majority of the lower-level clerks and secretaries were Africans and a few Indians. In that culture of inequality in the work force, the playing field for Indians in government was in no way equal.

When I attended evening classes at the Polytechnic Institute, I met the affable Reynold E. T. Francis. He worked at the Ministry of Agriculture and had recently built a new house near my home off Santa Cruz Old Road. He commuted to his job in his new Hillman Minx automobile. For several months before I started driving Alick's car, Reynold and his wife, Sylvia, generously gave me free rides on mornings to work in Port of Spain. They got to know my family well, and we have remained friends throughout the years.

In an attempt to reciprocate their transportation generosity, I offered to drive them to the airport when they were migrating to Canada. I was honored when they accepted my offer, which in Trinidad is reserved for close relatives. However, on the farewell night before their departure, we partied late into the night, and I did not wake up early enough to get them to the airport in good time. Reynold and Sylvia were all packed and ready for an exciting journey to Canada, but little did they know that the trip to the airport was going to be even more filled with drama. The mad rush required running red lights and stop signs and parking illegally. But they caught the flight to Canada, and our friendship was saved.

Reynold and Sylvia are retirees residing in Ottawa, Canada. From time to time, they visit relatives in Miami, where we meet to reminisce on our near fifty-year-old friendship. Reynold loves to tell the story of how my father anointed their firstborn baby son, Joel, when they vacationed in Trinidad and visited my parents. It was one of Papa's traditions to anoint the newborns of our family.

Reynold and Sylvia are English scholars who helped in editing the manuscript of this book. Not only are they qualified to edit my memoir, but they also have firsthand knowledge of my family's pioneering introduction of Deen's Doubles to the San Juan and Port of Spain areas in the early 1950s.

Grace

On April 1, 1965, a new, eighteen-year-old employee came to work in my department. Her name was Grace Cynthia Ramsingh. She was the most beautiful petite lass I had ever set eyes on. She was dressed in a light-blue, two-piece outfit. From the moment I saw her, I was love-struck and declared to my buddies, "OK, fellas, she is mine!" and I was not making an April fool's joke.

The clerical employees were in a large open space with rows of desks. Grace was about two desks away in front of me but positioned so I had a side view of her face. Even if I did not intend to stare at her, my physical location gave me no choice but to peruse her beautiful face, which stirred my emotions every time I looked up from my work. She caught me many times staring at her like an artist studying the details of a beautiful woman whose portrait he is painting. She became self-conscious and uncomfortable with my admiring gaze. I had already possessed her in my mind—it was love at first sight.

We spoke casually, but she was, of course, totally unaware of the effect she was having on my excited heart, which was pounding rapidly, like the sound of the dholak in a fast chutney song. She lived in Saint James and commuted to and from work by taxi. The short distance allowed her to go home for lunch daily, which eliminated any possibility of a luncheon date. An after-work date was also out of the question, as she was expected to be home by a certain time.

Since I wasn't able to have any private time with Grace, I figured out a plan to get some one-on-one time with her. Alick had bought his first automobile, a two-door British-made Anglia. The body was blue and the roof white. He did not have his driver's license yet, so I became his chauffeur, taking both of us to work in Port of Spain. One day I borrowed the car and told the most productive lie in my life: I told Grace I was going to Bournes Road, which was near her home, to visit an imaginary relative and offered her a ride—which she accepted! I was so elated that I felt the car was running on my high emotions instead of high octane. To have her enter that car was to have her enter my life.

When I dropped her off in front of her home on the northwest corner of Delhi and Bengal Streets, her mother was on the front porch witnessing the delivery of my precious passenger. Without hesitation, she asked Grace all the pertinent questions about me and my family, which Grace could not answer because all she knew about me was my name and that I worked with her in the same office. My Doubles background and double life had never entered our previous chats because I did not want anything to jeopardize the budding possibilities.

Her mother scolded her for accepting a ride from someone whose background check was incomplete. I returned to Port of Spain to pick up Alick for our drive home, having successfully accomplished my heart's mission. I still believe that to lie because of love is the best lie to tell, so I do not feel guilty in telling her about my fictitious relatives on Bournes Road.

Like me, she was the seventh of nine siblings, except they were six girls and three boys, while we were six boys and three girls. They were of Hindu origin, with all the children converted to Christianity, mainly to benefit from society's partiality to Christians in education and employment. In contrast, we remained Muslims who followed the faith loosely.

Grace's home was an impressive two-story building with all the modern amenities, such as telephone, radiogram, black-and-white television, comfortable living-room furniture, dedicated dining room, refrigerator, stove, washing machine, and indoor plumbing—a novelty in my world. Her father had a luxurious blue four-door Ford Fairlane automobile parked in their opened car port. Her parents' material wealth was conspicuous, especially to a boy from the Doubles Kitchen whose only wealth was in his ambitious dreams and his spirituality. The value of their car alone was worth more than my parents' humble house, where I lived. It was intimidating to think of how our two worlds could intersect because I was afraid of rejection based on class discrimination. But the love I was feeling for Grace emboldened me to throw caution to the tropical winds and pursue my heart's desire.

Grace's father was a home builder who purchased lands, developed the infrastructure, and built houses that were in great demand. His building projects were mainly in middle- and upper-middle-class areas of Diego Martin and Saint James. In addition, he owned several residential and commercial buildings that were leased to tenants. He was a millionaire before I understood what real affluence was.

Grace invited me to a picnic with some of her school friends at the botanical gardens in Port of Spain on a beautiful Sunday afternoon. She had prepared a picnic basket for the outing. I borrowed Alick's car again for my first exciting date with her. I picked her up at her parents' home and headed toward the botanical gardens on the northern side of the Queen's Park Savannah. I was not interested in meeting her friends and persuaded her to go to another location, where we could have a private picnic. We went up the Lady Chancellor Road to a spot overlooking the Emperor Valley Zoo and the Queen's Park Savannah. There we ate the goodies she had in her picnic basket, chatted, held hands, and experienced our first kiss—when I tasted the intoxicating nectar of her sweet lips. I felt certain that my feelings for her were being reciprocated, and all my fantasies of falling in love with her were rapidly becoming a reality. At sundown the picnic ended, but our lives together had only just begun.

Catalyst for Change

I bought a car shortly afterward from Rudy, one of Alick's brothers, for TT$2,100. It was a manual stick shift, British-made, four-door Hillman Minx, white in color and with the license plate number PH 2950. I paid for it with a loan from my father and some savings from my monthly salary. This was the first automobile in the Deen family, which had owned only bicycles before. Cabil was the only other sibling to have had a driver's license; throughout their lives, my parents never drove an automobile. Modern transportation technology had finally arrived at our home, and I felt a sense of pride that I was the catalyst for this change.

From her frequent visits to Mount Saint Benedict, Ma observed that many people got their new cars blessed by the priests there. She insisted that I go with her to have my car blessed. One of her favorite priests prayed and sprinkled holy water on us and the car. He gave me a Saint Christopher medal on a chain for safe travel. I hung it on the rear-view mirror.

Often I would run into Papa riding his freight bike on his way home from Port of Spain after his day's sales. I would transfer his Doubles box from the freight bike into the trunk of my car so he could ride home with less effort.

Lyra posing with my first automobile

With my high-school education, white-collar job, and automobile, I became the de facto leader in the family for which I felt a self-imposed responsibility. That became a function of my success—the more successful I became, the more responsible I felt toward my parents and siblings. They valued and welcomed my advice and input in their lives. Working in the family business together created the strong bond that we surviving siblings cherish. This strong sibling bond is what motivated Edool and Shamal to come from Winnipeg to my rescue from Hurricane Andrew, sparing no expense; it is what compelled me to leave Miami to be at Shamal's bedside throughout the night at the Eric Williams Medical Center where he was having a life-threatening surgery; and it's why Sharm was present in Miami when I was hospitalized in November 2012, just two weeks after she had lost Alick, who passed away on October 15, 2012.

Trepidations of Class Discrimination

I was very nervous when I first told Grace about Deen's Doubles. I felt like I was confessing a sin and apologizing for who I was. However, it had no impact on her—first, because she did not know the product, and second, her feelings for me had blinded her to any extraneous details of my life. I had captured her heart, which did not beat for materialism but for genuine love. Ever since she learned about Deen's Doubles, she has admired the originality and independence of my family and was attracted to those qualities in me.

I started to give her frequent rides home after work. She eventually invited me in to meet her parents. With my government job, my wearing a necktie, my proper English, and now with my automobile, I felt supremely qualified to approach the affluent Ramsingh family. However, the fear of class discrimination that accompanied me like my shadow made me nervous about exposing the fact that I was a son of the Doublesman. I thought such a revelation could jeopardize my budding relationship with Grace.

The nervousness of being introduced to her parents was exacerbated by her father's choosing that exact time to clean his shotgun. It was the most potent nonverbal communication I would ever experience. I was witnessing how action can really speak louder than words. I took it as a "wife or death" threat. Needless to say, it was a short and awkward visit.

When Grace's parents eventually found out about my Doubles background, they felt their desire for a successful future for their daughter was now being challenged. Like most parents, they wanted the "best" for their daughter. My invisible backpack, which now included insecurities from my impoverished background, made me wonder about my ability to provide the material comforts to which she had grown accustomed. But my charm and her parents' own humble origins made them see my human potential rather than my impoverished origin. They saw my future, not my past.

My fear that I might be unsuitable for Grace was beginning to materialize when she started to talk about her earlier desire to further her academic studies in Winnipeg, Manitoba, Canada. I interpreted her renewed interest in going to Canada as her having second thoughts about our relationship.

My humiliation at just the thought of being rejected by her felt worse than my insecurities.

She had a sister in Winnipeg whose husband was attending the University of Manitoba, so the move would have been easy for her. Another older sister was married to a veterinarian and was living in Chicago. Two older brothers and another sister were married and living in Saint Croix, US Virgin Islands, and making significant material progress. There was no doubt that this family was upwardly mobile. So, from a materialistic point of view, I wondered what a son of the Doublesman could ever offer a millionaire's daughter.

The thought of losing Grace started to manifest itself in a psychosomatic reaction of vitiligo on my lips and neck. Vitiligo is a skin condition in which the pigmentation of the skin is lost. It is especially devastating to people of color when these unsightly white spots contrast with dark skin. Vitiligo received global attention when Michael Jackson divulged that he had the skin condition. Cosmetically, it is disfiguring. It was certainly not the lighter skin pigmentation that was favored for upward social mobility. I believe that the stress of losing my first love was certainly a causal factor in my vitiligo condition. The anxiety I experienced thinking about my face becoming disfigured exacerbated the condition and made it unbearable. I knew that my intelligence and my handsome face were my main shields to deflect rejections, but now with my face in jeopardy, I felt disarmed and vulnerable.

I was extremely lucky to have Dr. Harry Bissoondath, a general practitioner in San Juan, show interest in my vitiligo condition. He prescribed what was at the time an experimental drug named Trisoralen, which is used in combination with an ultraviolet lamp to treat the condition. After several months of treatment, pigmentation started to return to the white spots, and eventually my skin regained all of the lost brown pigmentation. I was never happier to be in my own brown skin. It was a close call!

I had luckily succeeded in eliminating a likely reason for rejection—a disfigured face—but there was no medicine to cure the other reason for my insecurity: my Doubles background. I was desperately searching for the silver lining that must exist behind this dark cloud over my self-confidence and self-esteem. I knew that being poor did not mean I was ordinary, so I clung to the wings of my ambitions to excel and succeed in overcoming my insecurity.

With motivated confidence, I told Grace that if she was going to Winnipeg, I would be on the same plane with her. I immediately started the process of obtaining my passport and applying to schools in Winnipeg. When Grace told her parents about my decision to go to school in Winnipeg and not be geographically separated from the love of my life, they knew then I was dead serious about my relationship with her.

Her decision to go to Canada was in fact the transformative moment of my life. It made me seriously consider higher education in another land. It made our relationship stronger and motivated me to look beyond the horizon for a life without scorn, humiliation, and shame; to look beyond the social myopia of judging human potential based on one's birth circumstances.

My persistence paid off. I was promoted to the "green bench" at her house, which was the secluded lovers' seat on which her three elder sisters were courted before their respective marriages. It was situated between the eastern side of the house and the concrete fence facing Bengal Street. The shrub-bery along the fence provided a natural canopy of privacy from the street. Every day after work, I would drive Grace home and spend the early evenings with her on the green bench. It was on the green bench that I told her I wanted her to be the mother of our children. There we planned and fantasized about our lives together in Canada. I had won not only her heart but also her parents' approval!

As a socially ambitious young man, I believed education was the only window of opportunity for me to jump through to escape the wood-burning fires and smoke of the Doubles Kitchen that continued to suffocate me as I attempted to cross the social-class barriers in my aspirations to become upwardly mobile. I understood that education was the most effective tool to facilitate my upward social mobility. I sensed that it was only I who could pick myself up by the bootstraps and choose my outcomes, and not let my future depend on anyone's biased review of my past and make me a victim of it. This must be the perpetual struggle in the Indian caste system when a lower-caste person attempts to escape the caste of his or her birth and finds the pathways to prosperity filled with detours.

C. L. R. James, in his book *The Life of Captain Cipriani: An Account of British Government in the West Indies,* described Trinidad's social dynamics in these words:

> There are the nearly-white hanging on tooth and nail to the fringes of white society, and these, as is easy to understand, hate contact with the darker skin far more than some of the broader-minded whites. Then there are the browns, intermediates who cannot by any stretch of imagination pass as white but who will

not go one inch toward mixing with people darker than themselves. And so on, and on, and on.

In the prevailing multitiered social dynamics of Trinidad, it was more difficult for a non-Christian Indian from the lowest rung to climb the social ladder rapidly in public service, banking, and corporate employment despite his or her merit. The societal norms around race and class dynamics and the ascribed roles in the workplace must have contributed significantly to driving Indians to become independent small-business people. Entrepreneurship seemed to have been imposed on them.

In the complex social milieu of Trinidad, the aspiration to upward social mobility was a vague ambition for someone like me from an illiterate Muslim Indian family that was peddling Doubles for a living. I had to find a course of least resistance. The idea of going to Canada was an exciting option; I would be near the girl of my dreams and would pursue a higher education that I was sure would eliminate any social barriers.

At that time in Canada, if you were not white, you were black. I felt it would be easier to face "one dominant group" in Canada instead of Trinidad's hierarchy of dominant groups and subgroups. I was choosing between being a visible minority in a white person's country and an invisible minority in my own country. In short, I was choosing my discriminators. Going to Canada would be my silent protest against the employment inequality in my homeland and would also be an opportunity to change it. Cultures don't change overnight, and I was not going to wait for someone else to change things for me. I was determined to jump on this opportunity and take control of my life. In a leap of faith,

I hinged my hopes on Canada, where I believed I could live anonymously and where my merit would be more important than my ascribed lowly Doubles background. The risk of going to Canada where I could escape from shame seemed like a reasonable safety net.

As our courtship progressed, I took Grace to my humble home to meet my parents and siblings. The whole family was as nervous as I was to have a princess visit a pauper's abode. We spent most of the time on my front porch, enjoying the fresh air and looking out at the mountains that face my house in the distance.

The porch definitely offered much more to the senses than the pungent smell of spices emanating from the congested Doubles Kitchen with all its Doubles paraphernalia. There were the blackened walls and roof surrounding the large wood-burning firesides that created much smoke, the huge pots and pans, bags of inventory of chickpeas and flour, firewood, and other materials. The two freight bikes with their Doubles Boxes were parked in the area. In the midst of this organized congestion were a hammock, a wooden bunk bed, and a small table that my parents used for rest and recuperation from the exertions of producing Doubles. My mother preferred the hammock and my father the bunk bed, which he built from scrap wood. He built the head of the bunk elevated to minimize his snoring. It was not upholstered, just covered with a piece of canvas-like material. Its surface was hard but good for his tired back, he would say. The pungent smell of curry and other spices permeated the air around the house. In the front yard, in full view, was always a huge pile of firewood used for fuel in the production process. The firewood was discarded lumber that sawmills sold cheaply.

Sharm offered us soft drinks, and I prayed that Grace would not drink too much to make her want to pee in our outhouse—the ultimate symbol of our poverty that seemed to justify my shame.

Ma and Papa resting in the Doubles Kitchen

Jamaloo, Shamal, Edool, and I were determined to elevate the social status of our family in the community, and we made that objective our lifelong mission. Our desire to make meaning of our lives was a passion born of adversity; we did not want just to survive our circumstances, we drove ourselves to rise above them.

In the ensuing years, Jamaloo replaced the freight bikes with pickups and station wagons and built an impressive house for his family. Shamal, the born entrepreneur, was determined to bring dignity to Doubles by taking it off the streets and providing "proper housing" for the business. Edool was already attending high school and appreciating the opportunities that education could present. He and I were obsessed with reversing society's image of the Doubles-man through education. We didn't just fight our way through our circumstances but were determined to create better lives because of the struggle.

I sent from Canada the first large patio umbrella for use over the Doubles Box in the San Juan location and encouraged my parents to buy their first Hobart flour mixer. I replaced the wood used as fuel for frying baras with a round propane gas burner (seen in the picture below). I had it installed in the same fireside where the frying process took place. It was the first time Ma and Papa were able to enjoy the luxury of heat without smoke in their daily frying of baras.

Later on I had a four-burner stove on legs custom-built for boiling the chana. This transition from wood to gas was a little tricky because when chana is boiled in high heat, it froths and boils over the pots, dripping into the wood-burning fireside. Papa thought the dripping would ruin the gas burn-ers, thus making his wood-burning fireside more practical. But the way I designed the gas stove protected the burners from the drippings, and after some reluctance and keeping his wood-burning fireside as a backup, Papa finally relented to going 100 percent gas and gave up wood as a fuel source. The wood-burning firesides were so much a part of him that he was experiencing separation anxiety in letting them go. If there is one notable contribution I made to Deen's Doubles, it would be the elimination of smoke from the production process; it was a milestone in the evolution of the industry.

Papa and Ma endured some forty years of wood-smoke inhalation, unaware of the health hazards. They were so focused on their production goals that they threw caution to the smoky winds and prayed for good health. Recent research raises new concerns about the toxic substances in wood smoke. Scientists say that "the tiny airborne specks of pollution carry carcino-genic chemicals deep into lungs and trigger DNA damage and gene changes. Exposure to the particulates in smoke irritates the lungs and air passages, causing swelling that obstructs breath-ing. Wood smoke can worsen asthma, and is especially harmful to children and older people. It also has been linked to respi-ratory infections, adverse changes to the immune system, and early deaths among people with cardiovascular or lung prob-lems." (Source: Environmental Health News published by Envi-ronmental Health Sciences, March 14, 2011 by Cheryl Katz.)

MamooDeen and Rasulan frying baras

Wedding Bells

Badru and Grace, July 28, 1968

In January 1968, when Grace was twenty and I was twenty-two, we got engaged to be married at her parents' home in the presence of our families. Six months later we were joined in blissful matrimony. For the religious satisfaction of our respective parents, we had a small, unofficial Muslim ceremony at my home on Friday, July 26, 1968, and on Sunday, July 28, 1968, exchanged official marriage vows at the Saint Agnes Anglican church in Saint James.

July 26 seemed to be a fateful date for my parents, who had lost Habil, their firstborn, on that very date twelve years earlier. My getting married and leaving the security of their home was an emotional loss for both them and me. The feeling of leaving my close-knit family, to whom I had brought so much pride, was bittersweet. Caught between two loves, my family came in second. I felt like I was deserting my team midstream when our social struggles were still unfinished.

Sharm designed and made Grace's beautiful wedding dress. Our flower girls were Sharm's daughter, Lyra, and Indra, Grace's baby sister. The maid of honor was Grace's sister Joyce, and her friend Judy was her bridesmaid. My cousin Azard Gopaul was my best man.

On the day of the church wedding, when we were all hurriedly getting ready at my home for the big occasion, Dood, my belligerent brother-in-law wanted me to give him a haircut. Because of the time constraints and the mad rush to get everyone ready, I refused his request. He was upset and started to raise his voice, when Alick shouted at him from his room at the back of the house, admonishing him to behave himself. Dood wasted no time in trying to enter Alick's room to start a physical fight. Jamaloo and others tried to restrain

him, and in the melee Dood grabbed at my elegantly deco-
rated groom's wedding cake, ruining it. Jamaloo, visibly dis-
turbed, took the cake and smashed it on Dood's face. The
icing must have tasted better than the shaving cream he was
demanding.

Dood, embarrassed and realizing that he was overpow-
ered, displaced his aggression on his wife, my sister Subrattan. Once again he abused her physically and denied her
the pleasure of seeing Grace and me get married. She had
to watch my wedding automobile procession to the church
from a distance, like an uninvited guest.

The reception was held at Grace's home and was attended
by many guests from both sides of our families. We had the
Javo Brothers live band playing music. We had Indo-Trin-
idad cuisine with curry goat and paratha roti and an open
bar. Mr. Wilson, my secondary school principal, and his wife,
as well as our supervisor from the Treasury, attended. The
few hours of celebrating our wedding temporarily brought
illiterate cake-fighting Doubles folks, professionals, educated
people, and rich folks to break roti together.

We spent our honeymoon on the sister isle of Tobago
and returned for a short stay at Grace's parents' home before
starting our lives together.

Chapter 11: O Canada

One month after our wedding, on August 30, 1968, we both left Trinidad for Winnipeg "on the same plane." A large entourage of family and friends came to see us off at the Piarco Airport. In my youthful excitement to start my life in a new country with Grace, I did not fully consider the effect my departure would have on my parents. They were "losing" a third son—two to the angel of death and one to Cupid. It was the first time I could recall that my undemonstrative father hugged me and gave me his blessings. My mother was extremely sad to see me go. They were worried that if we were not successful in Canada, they would not be in a financial position to rescue us and thought we were possibly making a mistake by abandoning our "good jobs in the Treasury."

Grace's parents generously paid for our airfares and gave us financial gifts as well. My parents gave us TT$100 (US $50), the most they could have afforded. To me, their monetary gift was not as important as the opportunity they gave me to aspire to accomplish my dreams. Our ambitions exceeded our combined savings and financial gifts, totaling C$1,400, with which we began our marital lives in Canada. When compared with the pair of chickens, a goat, and a bicycle that my parents started their marriage with, our initial cash asset was indeed a major improvement. Once we left Trinidad, we were determined to make it on our own and not be a burden on our parents, especially mine.

Our flights to Winnipeg were via New York and Toronto with BWIA and Air Canada. We missed our connecting flight from Toronto to Winnipeg because of immigration delays in processing our visas and finally arrived in Winnipeg to begin our independence from our parents at 3:00 a.m. on August 31, 1968, which coincided with the sixth anniversary of Trinidad and Tobago's independence from British rule. The excitement of our first international trip to discover a new country together as honeymooners made us oblivious of the long delays in reaching our destination.

We stayed with Grace's sister and brother-in-law for a few weeks until an apartment on the first floor in the same building at 1-682 Corydon Avenue became available. The rent was $65 per month, which we found a little steep, so I invited my cousin and best man in my wedding, Azard Gopaul, to share the apartment for a third of the cost. He stayed with us for ten months while attending the Red River Community College.

Everything was new to us in Winnipeg. It was our city to discover and possess. It was an organized society with clean streets where people would queue to enter the buses, unlike the pushing I was used to in Trinidad. All vehicles were left-hand drive and driven on the right side of the roads—the complete opposite of Trinidad, which followed the British system of driving. I soon discovered that pedestrians subconsciously follow the same rules of vehicular traffic and walk on pavements accordingly. So, coming from Trinidad, where I was used to walking on the left side of the pedestrian pavements, I kept running into approaching Canadian pedestrians who were normally walking on the right side of the pavements. I had to adapt to the flow of vehicular and pedestrian traffic quickly.

It was easy to adapt to the organized and efficient city of Winnipeg, where I would soon take for granted the telephones that always worked, the water that always flowed in the taps, the electricity that was always on, and the buses that ran like clockwork. The work ethic in the city was noticeably more efficient than what I was used to seeing. I was flabbergasted to see beautiful blue-eyed, blonde girls pumping gas at the fuel stations. In Trinidad the social hierarchy of race and skin pigmentation would have made such employment impossible.

Winnipeg, the capital of the province of Manitoba, has the vantage point of being at the center of the North American continent. Manitoba, with a total area of 250,950 square miles, is 135 times the size of Trinidad, which is only 1,864 square miles. In fact, Lake Winnipeg, which is 9,465 square miles in surface area, is five times larger than the island of Trinidad. However, the population of Manitoba in 1968 was just under one million inhabitants, with Winnipeg comprising over half the province's population. The population of Trinidad and Tobago in 1968 was larger than Manitoba's, with just over one million inhabitants.

We struggled with the harsh cold of the long winters that would see temperatures plunge to minus forty degrees Celsius and many times lower with the wind chill factor. Winnipeg has rightfully earned the nickname "Winterpeg."

The long, cold winters made me a better student by forcing me to remain indoors, where I focused more on my studies.

I had been accepted to the Red River Community College in Winnipeg to study radio operating and electronic communications, but on arrival I switched to the Winnipeg Adult Education Center to study for grade twelve, which was the prerequisite for entering university. I saved a year by not doing A-levels in Trinidad, which was the alternative prerequisite for Canadian university entry.

All the textbooks at the Winnipeg Adult Education Center were loaned to the students, which was an unexpected boon for my limited budget. I wanted to study medicine but hated chemistry and so did not pursue it. I graduated from grade twelve and was accepted to the University of Manitoba (UM) for the fall semester of 1969 to begin a four-year bachelor of commerce (honors) program.

Our financial strategy to survive in Canada while obtaining my university education was for me to work in the summers to cover tuition, textbooks, and supplies, and for income from Grace's anticipated employment to cover living expenses.

Summer Jobs

At the start of summer of 1969, a fellow Trinidadian and grade-twelve graduate, Roop Dass, and I went to the immigration office to obtain temporary work permits. The officer who interviewed Roop granted him a work permit, but the one I went to denied my application. When we compared the outcomes of our interviews, I told him I was going back to see the officer who handled his request. Roop was scared that his work permit would be rescinded if I exposed the inconsistency in the rulings, so he disappeared. I presented myself as a new applicant to the officer who attended to Roop, and without hesitation he granted me a work permit for the summer of 1969. I almost became a victim of the arbitrary application of the rules, which could have changed the entire course of my life. Without that summer's income, I would not have been able to pay the tuition for the upcoming school year at UM.

Being waiters or porters on the Canadian National Railways (CN) were the jobs of choice for foreign students on the Canadian prairies. I landed a waiter position with CN, and in no time I was trained to balance large trays of food on my fingertips as the train swayed and rocked along its track at sixty miles per hour.

The work on the trains was the nearest thing to military service I could have imagined. We were shouted out of our bunk beds at 5:00 a.m. and returned to the crew car between 10:00 and 11:00 p.m., only to repeat the routine the next day. After my first day's work, my untrained muscles were going into spasms, and my coworker and friend Ken Nanan gave me a massage with a very potent liniment to relieve the soreness and pain. When you get off the train you continue to feel the rocking back and forth even while standing still. The 'clickity-clack' sound continues to resonate throughout your body for several hours after disembarking the train. My route was Western Canada, from Winnipeg to Vancouver with an occasional trip to Churchill on the Hudson Bay in Northern Manitoba.

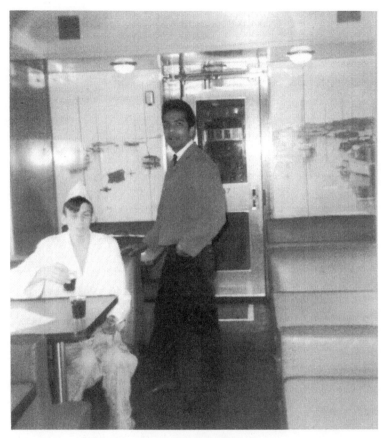

The author (R) as a waiter on Canadian National Railways

Once my 110-pound body adapted to the physical demands of the eighteen-hour days, I started to appreciate the opportunity to "be paid to explore Canada." The journey across the Canadian prairies from Winnipeg to Calgary can be monotonous, but I was always amazed at the great expanse of land mass used for agriculture, growing wheat, pulses, and other grains that feed the world. From the train windows, I could see where wheat, chickpeas, yellow split peas, and coriander are grown—the very ingredients of Doubles and roti. In Trinidad, yellow split peas are used for the Indian dhals and our famous dhalpouri. I felt a certain affinity to this land and realized that Trinidadians are gastronomically connected to the Canadian prairies.

The majestic Canadian Rockies span nearly 69,500 square miles across two provinces: Alberta and British Columbia. Along the breathtaking scenery from Calgary to Vancouver the train snakes through the majestic wilderness and the quiet alpine towns of Banff, Lake Louise, Jasper and Kamloops. The many waterfalls seem to disturb the tranquility of the magnificent vistas that appear untouched by man. Bears, elk, moose and big-horn mountain goats roam these rugged canyons. Signs of civilization are so few that I felt like an explorer seeing the great Rocky Mountains for the first time. Traversing this expanse of pristine natural beauty, where the pine-scented atmosphere encourages deep breathing, made me oblivious of the demanding work as a waiter on the many trips I made over the Canadian Rockies.

Luckily, Grace accepted this sacrifice we made to succeed, including spending our first wedding anniversary apart—with her on the prairie and me in the Rockies. On my weekly trips, she interacted with her sister, brother-in-law, and their two children. Having relatives nearby minimized the guilt I felt for being so far away from her.

My tuition fees for my first year at UM were secured, and I used the tips of about $900 I earned to purchase our first automobile in Canada. It was a preowned red 1966 VW Beetle that cost us $700. The location of the engine in the rear gave the car great traction in the snow and minimized the treacherous driving conditions in winter. Several of my Caribbean friends took their driving tests with this vehicle.

Maybe it was my father's charismatic salesmanship that I inherited that made me excel as a waiter on the CN trains serving the public. No doubt, my personality was a function of the amount of tips I could generate. The effective income of wages plus tips was excellent for a student's summer job. The joy of coming home after the train trips and counting my cash tips was similar to my father's counting the coins at the end of the day's sale of Doubles.

The job on the trains was great for single males or married men who enjoyed being away from their wives. I was neither; I could not wait to be home with Grace. As a result, for the next three summers, I decided to find summer jobs nearer to our home in Winnipeg so Grace and I could enjoy the short summers together after those long, cold Winnipeg winters.

The Factor's Table

Canadian National Railways built vast landmark hotels-castles to draw the rich and the royal in several major cities across Canada. In Winnipeg it was the Fort Garry Hotel, located on Broadway between Fort and Garry Streets close to the CN Railway Station. Built in 1913, it was designated as a National Historic Site of Canada in 1981. The château-style twelve-story building is 192 feet tall and originally held 340 rooms. It was named after the nearby Upper Fort Garry, which stood at the junction of the Red and Assiniboine Rivers. Over the decades its prominence attracted dozens of famous personalities who enjoyed the hotel's hospitality. Guests included Nat King Cole, Victor Borge, Lawrence Olivier, Joan Crawford, Liberace, Mantovani, Tommy Dorsey, Louis Armstrong, Benny Goodman, Jack Dempsey, Bobby Hull, Field Marshall Montgomery, several prime ministers including Lester Pearson, and King George VI and Queen Elizabeth. They all dined in the high-end restaurant of the hotel called the Factor's Table. Mr. Freddy Nyquest was the maître d'.

With contrived confidence I entered this palatial hotel, where doormen in coattails, top hats, and white gloves held doors with shiny brass handles open for the upper crust of society. The floor of the lobby was intimidating with its shiny marble, and the Factor's Table restaurant was heavily plush-carpeted. I chose the downtime between the end of lunch and the start of dinner to approach Mr. Nyquest. I convinced him that with minimum training I could transfer my knowledge of serving as a waiter on the CN trains to a waiter in a top CN hotel restaurant.

Freddy took an immediate liking to me and employed me as a waiter for the next three summers and during Christmas breaks as well. All of my university tuition fees were now secured. Freddy treated me as a father would, and I saw in him great similarities with Papa. Though worlds apart, they both were people satisfying the hunger of the public. The difference was my father was satisfying the hunger of poor customers from his Doubles Box, while Freddy was satiating the gastronomic delights of affluent elites in the Factor's Table. They both had a passion for feeding the hungry.

The Fort Garry Hotel, Winnipeg Manitoba

University of Manitoba

Founded in1877, the University of Manitoba (UM) was the first university of western Canada. In 1969 it was one of the top tertiary educational institutions in Canada with about fifteen thousand students in over a dozen faculties. I was unaware at the time that this was the university that James West attended from 1957 to 1964 and where he obtained his BA and CA degrees. The coincidence was striking, since my mother had wished for me to follow in his footsteps. I enrolled in the Faculty of Management (now called Asper School of Business), which was established in 1937, to pursue the bachelor of commerce (honors) degree.

Having uneducated parents who could not capitalize on the Doubles industry that they created, I was motivated to study business management to vindicate their handicap.

Since almost all the first-year students were young high school graduates, not only was I older than most but I was among the few who were married. Living off campus and being married did not give me the university experience that young single students see as the best years of their lives. My years at UM were too focused on work to be enjoyable. My mission was to make up for lost time and get qualified academically to hold a lucrative position of respect and pride for me, Grace, and my folks back in Trinidad. I could not disappoint the entourage that had wished me luck at Piarco Airport when we departed for Canada.

The first semester of the four-year commerce program was very challenging for me. I was inundated with the course load, and for the first time felt out of my league academically. Nothing in my background or experience had prepared me for the challenges of an honors business degree. I decided to change my strategy. The four-year bachelor of commerce (honors) program could also be completed in two years after an undergraduate degree. So, I decided to switch to a degree in economics and sociology and then return to the two-year commerce honors program. The BA in economics and a

BComm (Hons) would give me a wider academic training and provide a competitive edge in the job market.

Few Caribbean students were at UM, and they were mainly from Trinidad. It was easy to bond and become friends with them as we all shared a common ambition of improving ourselves academically in a foreign land. In most of my classes, I was the only visible minority student. Between classes I would seek out Trinidadians, whose funny disposition always put me at ease. The friendships I made at UM have lasted a lifetime.

At nights and on weekends, Grace would type my assignments and term papers on our used manual Royal portable typewriter. It was tedious work for her, especially after her regular day job. However, she became an active partner in my academic pursuits. She shared all my anxieties in awaiting the grades for those assignments and term papers, which she felt were her own after meticulously typing them. Luckily, most of the grades for those typewritten assignments were cause for celebration. Grace and I were working as a team to change the course of our lives, just as my parents had with the limited resources available to them in Princes Town, Trinidad.

Our survival strategy in Canada caused Grace to selflessly postpone her own academic ambitions for the welfare of our partnership. She exhibited selfless traits similar to what my mother had done. Grace patiently waited until the 1980s, when the second of our two children entered school, before enrolling in Miami-Dade Community College to pursue her associate in science degree in fashion design. In

1987, the year of her graduation, the faculty in the Fashion Department selected her as their outstanding student of the year. Her personal sacrifice was the foundation on which my progress and that of our children was built and sustained. Our two children and I are extremely lucky to be blessed with such a devoted mother and wife. We owe all of our successes to her, our amazing Grace.

Edool

When I saw the opportunities on the other side of the educational door, I decided to leave it open for Edool, so he could make the transition as well from limited means to unlimited opportunities. It was the same as when my father saw the opportunities that Doubles offered and invited his two brothers-in-law to experience his vision.

Edool had just graduated from high school in Trinidad and was considering his options. Jobs were scarce, and he did not have a James West to help him find one. The family Doubles business was always there as a safety net for him, but with his high school education, he was also thinking outside the Doubles Box. I was able to convince him that despite the cold weather in Winnipeg, greater opportunities existed there to work part time while attending school. I was extremely happy when he accepted the challenge of a new life in Winnipeg with Grace and me.

In 1970 I obtained a job offer from Scott National in Winnipeg to help sponsor Edool for his resident status in Canada. Greg Tuttle, a Canadian friend from my grade-twelve class, knew the general manager of Scott National, and this contact facilitated my obtaining the job offer for Edool.

For the two years before Edool came to Winnipeg, I had not seen my parents or siblings. I had not even heard their voices because they did not have a telephone. I felt guilty for leaving them trapped in the smoke-filled heat of the Doubles Kitchen while I freely explored other possibilities in a world that was alien to them. I was missing the human interaction with loved ones that had sustained me for so long. I wrote let-tergrams—the cheapest form of communication—to them to report on our progress in Winnipeg. They would receive my lettergrams but had to wait for Jamaloo or Shamal to come home to read them. Sometimes when they became anxious to hear the contents of the lettergrams, they would ask strang-ers to read them. To solve this communication problem, I provided them with a cassette recorder, and we exchanged "voice mails" for the rest of the time I spent in Canada. If only there had been Skype!

The bonus from these recordings was that when they had no more to say, Papa sang and recorded some of his favorite songs on the tapes for us. He kept the tempo of the songs by playing the dhantal while he sang. It's lucky he did this, because these are the only recordings we have of him sing-ing. I later added music to his vocals in a recording studio in Miami. On the CD recording, Rampersad Ramdass, the famous Trinidadian drummer, plays the tabla, my son Jeff plays percussion, and I play the keyboard and dhantal. One of songs on the recording is "Dila Gafil," a philosophical song on life and death that Papa sang at funerals. After his passing, this recorded song was poignantly played at the funerals of Ma and Subrattan.

When Edool arrived at the Winnipeg airport on Sunday, August 16, 1970, I was crying tears of joy to see my baby brother joining me in the academic struggle to rise above our circumstances, to change our lives' direction and leave behind the shame, ridicule, and stigma we were subjected to in Trinidad as sons of the Doublesman.

During the three years that Edool lived with us, he focused on obtaining his grade-twelve certification from the same Winnipeg Adult Education Center that I had attended and entered the Red River Community College, where he graduated in hotel/motel management. While he attended school, I got Freddy Nyquest to employ him on weekends and evenings at the Factor's Table in the Fort Garry Hotel. He proudly and independently supported himself throughout school with that job. During Christmas breaks and in the summers of 1971 and 1972, I worked with him at the Factor's Table. We were the dynamic Deen duo of the Factor's Table, and Freddy would place his best customers in our stations.

We had an interesting experience at the Factor's Table when a Trinidadian young man studying hotel management on a Trinidad government scholarship came on an immersion course to learn the service etiquette of fine dining. Imagine the contradiction of two sons of the Doublesman teaching the service etiquette of fine dining to someone who was being groomed for leadership of the Trinidad and Tobago Tourist Board!

After his graduation, Edool managed a few restaurants, including Bonanza Restaurants. He switched careers and became the manager of purchasing and food services in the Head Office of the Canadian Wheat Board in Winnipeg, where he was employed until his retirement.

Saint James, Trinidad, provided both Edool and me with our soul mates. In 1975, he married Zinny, a beautiful Trinidadian girl who emigrated to Winnipeg, Canada, from Saint James. They produced two wonderful daughters, Nadia and Natasha, who are both University of Manitoba graduates. Nadia is the youngest director of quality assurance and food safety to be appointed in the history of Richardson International, where she has been an integral part of making the firm an internationally renowned and well respected leading food-safety and security-certified company. Natasha, the educator, is a high school science teacher.

For many years, Edool and Zinny were involved with the University of Manitoba's Home Stay Program for International Students and hosted students from over ten countries in their home.

Edool remains busy and productive in his retirement. He manages the vendor services of the Saint Norbert Farmers' Market on the outskirts of Winnipeg from June to October. The outdoor market provides small producers a marketing opportunity in a cooperative environment. His involvement with this market satisfies his nostalgic need to serve small vendors like his father and brothers in the San Juan Market in Trinidad, who did not have an organized cooperative infrastructure to improve their opportunities.

Edool's successful life in Canada is a cogent example of investing in opportunities for future prosperity. Education and hard work were the keys to rising above our circumstances and reversing the expectation of social stagnation. Education gave us the tools to succeed in Canada and opened worlds we did not know existed. Our potential to achieve our career goals in Canada was nurtured by a system based on merit that offered more opportunities than our beloved homeland. Similar to our ancestors who came from India to Trinidad, Edool, like me, accepted the challenge of a new vision for a new life in a new country.

The similar paths that our lives followed, away from the Doubles business to achieve our respective career goals, created a special bond that remains inseparable. We share and compare the vicissitudes of our lives and the lives of our families. We are genuinely happy for each other's successes and internalize the pains of setbacks. We are each other's confidant and literally our brother's keeper.

Shamal

My brother Shamal showed early signs of following in the entrepreneurial footsteps of our father. He, like my father and older brother Jamaloo, became immune to the shame that was consuming Edool and me. Shamal got more publicly involved in the Doubles business than Edool and I did. Our parents enrolled him in Bally's Commercial School in San Juan to take some accounting and bookkeeping courses in the hope that he, too, would rise above the difficult Doubles circumstances that did not offer an easy lifestyle.

At that school Shamal also endured the mocking and bullying of other students for being a son of the Doublesman.

Unlike Edool and me, who found refuge in education, Shamal relied on his entrepreneurial drive to overcome the peer put-downs. He saw the wisdom of being one's own boss, like our father, and chose to make and count his own money instead of attending Bally's Commercial School to become a book-keeper to count other people's money. Eventually the children who tried to ridicule him became his loyal customers.

With the help of our parents, he ventured out on his own to sell roti from a kiosk on the eastern side of the railway station in Port of Spain. At 5:00 a.m. each morning, he would take two taxis to get to Port of Spain, carrying fresh meats and vegetables for the preparation of his daily menus. The selling prices for potato and chicken rotis were fifteen and twenty-five cents, respectively. Inflation over the years has changed prices for these same products from cents to dollars.

Roti is a round, soft flatbread used as a wrap for curried meats and/or vegetables. The roti of choice for commercial purposes is the dhalpouri. It is made with ground, seasoned, parboiled yellow split peas placed inside the dough, which is then spread out like a tortilla and cooked on a hot oiled tawa.

Shamal's first venture was profitable enough to help him move to a more convenient location on Real Street, San Juan, where he and his wife, Claudette, and their baby, Shanu, lived on location at the take-out restaurant. As a non-Indian, Claudette quickly learned the roti and Doubles business, and like our mother, she became the propeller of the business. Their new location was a busy area with a high density of school-children, including those from Wilson's San Juan Secondary where Edool and I had been students.

This was the first location where Deen's Doubles were not sold from a Doubles Box on the streets. Unlike Edool and me, who became victims of shame, Shamal started on a life's mission to bring dignity to Doubles. He believed in his mission and was willing to work hard to be the best. He operated this location very successfully while continuing to help Papa and Jamaloo on weekends in the San Juan market.

Edool and I were adapting to the Canadian lifestyle in Winnipeg and started to encourage Shamal to emigrate to Canada, where we would attempt to re-create the communal security in family numbers. Freddy Nyquest signed a job offer that I wrote on a Fort Garry Hotel's letterhead and nominated Shamal, his wife, and their two children to Canada for landed immigrant status.

It was a major decision to close down a successful business and emigrate to the unknown, but Shamal and his young family were undaunted. They accepted the challenge and emigrated to Canada on April 14, 1975. Edool and I were following the professional path of corporate careers, which made our transition in Canada easier, but Shamal was an entrepreneur from a third-world country with specialized skills of producing roti and Doubles—food products that were unknown and too ethnic for the mainstream Canadian consumer…or so we thought.

With their life's savings from Trinidad, Shamal and Claudette bought a townhouse near us on Meadowood Drive, and he accepted the first job he could find—as a security guard. That assignment made him think he had made a mistake in coming to Canada. He quit the position in no time and started to work on the CN trains as a waiter/porter/cook, where he refined his skills in Canadian food preparation and customer service. Shortly afterward he sold the townhouse and bought a single-family house at 15 Brampton Street, Saint Vital, Winnipeg.

There was a Roco Gas Station on Sargent Avenue that was owned by a Trinidadian named Carl. On Saturdays a few Trinidadians and other Caribbean people would hang out there for the ethnic camaraderie the place offered. Shamal approached Carl and asked if he could bring some rotis to sell to these Caribbean folks, and Carl gave him the OK. So, on Saturdays when he was not on the train, he and Claudette made rotis that he sold out of a cooler at the Roco Gas Station. They were an instant hit, and some customers started placing orders in advance.

The experiment exceeded all expectations and gave him the confidence that he should get his own food outlet to sell rotis and Deen's Doubles in Winnipeg. Having experienced the joy of being his own boss, like our father, he knew he was never going to be happy as a wage slave. He sold his house and bought an existing restaurant on 205 Marion Street in the French enclave of Saint Boniface, Winnipeg. The restaurant was attached to the front of a two-story house with a full basement.

On December18, 1978, Shamal and Claudette opened Deen's Diner, where Deen's Doubles were offered on the menu as an appetizer to be eaten with knife and fork by white Canadian customers. Rotis and other Trinidadian dishes were the main items on the menu. He was the first to import Solo beverages from Trinidad to western Canada. Solo beverages are the nostalgic complementary drinks for Doubles and rotis. He was now closer to the source of the main ingredients in producing his ethnic cuisine. Flour, chickpeas, yellow split peas, and potatoes are grown in Manitoba and Saskatchewan. He imported from Trinidad spices and other ingredients for the condiments and seasonings.

Shamal had succeeded in elevating the status of Doubles and finally giving it the dignity that Deen's Doubles deserved. He made it possible for me and Edool to start reembracing our Doubles heritage.

Deen's Diner became so popular that it was featured in several newspapers and magazines, including Air Canada's *EnRoute* magazine. The success led them to acquire the property next door, and the two adjoining front yards were merged into one. They built a stage for live music bands and placed patio tables and umbrellas in an open-air setting under tall oak trees. They called it Deen's Calypso Gardens. It became the cultural hub for Caribbean people and the place of choice for visiting Trinidadians, including popular artists such as the Mighty Sparrow and Baron, among several others.

Shamal, Claudette, and their three children—Shanu, Laura, and Barbara—were cultural ambassadors who replicated a Trinidadian ambience in the middle of Canada some three thousand three hundred miles away from their homeland. At Deen's Diner and Deen's Calypso Gardens, Canadians in Winnipeg enjoyed the taste and sounds of Trinidad without having to leave home.

Deen's Calypso Gardens, Winnipeg

Our Firstborn Child

My first graduation in 1972, with a BA in economics and sociology, coincided with Grace's pregnancy with our first baby. The honeymoon was over and our homebuilding project had started. This added an urgency to become the full-time breadwinner for my young family, but I was torn between this responsibility and my academic objective. My personal challenge to return and complete the honors commerce program was of paramount importance. The degree would most certainly give me greater opportunities in the world of business. I decided to bite the bullet and go for the commerce degree.

Our future parental roles were as exciting to contemplate as was the career path I was dreaming of after my BComm

(Hons) degree. We started to imagine what the baby would look like and drew some sketches with Grace's full lips, my big eyes, her floppy ears, my big nose and unibrows. The images we created were hilarious. We had no prior knowledge of the baby's sex, so we selected tentative male and female names. Although the baby's first kicks were uncomfortable for Grace, they were my first physical interactions with our first-born, to whom we were speaking before birth. The unfolding miracle we were experiencing further strengthened the bonds of our partnership that we had embarked on five years earlier. Our anticipation was growing as fast as the baby's little heart beating inside of Grace. The experience brought us tremendous joy.

I accompanied Grace during her sixteen hours of labor at Victoria General Hospital, until the doctors entered for the delivery and I was required to leave. We were relieved that both Grace and the baby were out of danger and that it was a boy, whom we named Jeffrey Omar. He made his grand entrance on Thursday, January 4, 1973, at 11:09 p.m. The temperature that night fell to minus 26.6 °C, with the wind-chill factor taking it much lower. It was so cold that I had to leave my VW Beetle running so the small engine would not freeze up while awaiting Jeff's arrival. In 1973, C-sections were not as common as they are today, or Jeff would have been delivered earlier with less stress on him and Grace. It was the most exciting time of our married lives when Grace literally delivered on her promise—made on the green bench—to be the mother of our children.

Jeff's middle name, Omar, came from Omar Sharif, the handsome star of the movie *Dr. Zhivago*. Jeff weighed in at six pounds, three ounces, a big baby for the small-framed, petite Grace. Unlike the sketches we drew before he was born, he inherited our best physical features, plus a head full of black hair. He was an exceptionally handsome baby boy, just like his namesake Omar Sharif.

The next day I telephoned Grace's parents with the good news, and they had to relay the birth announcement to my parents personally since my parents had no telephone. We missed sharing this joyous moment with our extended families in Trinidad, and Grace certainly missed having her mother or a sister to provide the female support that is so appreciated at this time in a woman's life. My three sisters always felt comforted to be near Ma, especially for their first deliveries. This was the price we had to pay for our geographic separation from our loved ones in the pursuit of a "better" life.

Grace's sister and her family, who lived in Winnipeg when we first arrived there, had relocated to Calgary, so Edool was the only family support we had. However, our cultural norms, which did not include males on these occasions, kept him somewhat aloof until he became the first visitor two days later.

What an amazing experience it was to hold my firstborn son for the first time and wonder about life's miracle of birth. I tried to imagine what my father's thoughts were when he first held me in his arms. He must have thought, *Great, another male to perpetuate my Doubles legacy!* When I perused baby Jeff's face for the first time, I saw in his eyes the ambition that had hurled me into the first world. Like my father, I too was looking for continuity of my hopes and dreams. To look at Jeff's face was to see a new member of my team who was going to run our relay race out of illiteracy.

As a university graduate, in 1972 I was able to change our Canadian immigration status from student visas to permanent residents. Canada's immigration policy encouraged foreign students who graduated from Canadian universities to stay in Canada and become productive residents/citizens. Canada understood that to remain progressive it must attract this human capital, which was already within its borders, for its value in terms of creativity, intelligence, and drive.

In the summer of 1973, after completing one year of the two-year honors commerce program, I was employed by the Canadian federal government's Transport Ministry as a job analyst in the Winnipeg Personnel Department. At the end of my summer assignment, I was offered a full-time position as a job classification officer to replace my boss, who was being transferred to Ottawa. It was an extremely difficult decision I had to make. I was tempted to drop out of the final year of my commerce program and give Grace and our nine-month-old son a more comfortable life sooner, but I agonizingly chose to finish my last academic year to obtain my commerce degree.

I graduated with my BComm (Hons) degree in 1974—the same year Papa won $60,000 in the Trinidad national lottery. It was the largest financial lump sum he'd ever had. He shared some of his windfall with his children and his two sisters and used some of the funds to complete the construction of three rental-income properties he was having built in Grand Curacaye, Bourg Mulatresse. Before the windfall, he was buying building materials for the project piecemeal. Now he was able to speed up the completion of his investment, which would generate a passive income for their retirement years.

Grace's parents visited us in 1975 and were very pleased with our progress. We were still living in an apartment, which was somewhat restrictive for Jeff, who was then two years old. Having been so successful in real estate, they encouraged us to buy our first home and gave us the down payment for it. We bought a townhouse at 488 Meadowood Drive, Saint Vital, in a Winnipeg suburb. This wise investment in real estate served us well as we relocated several times during my career and upgraded our house each time from the proceeds of the appreciated value of the previous property.

Daddy's Girl

In the fall of 1975, Grace became pregnant with our second child. On Saturday, June 12, 1976, our beautiful daughter, Alisha Lori, was born at Victoria General Hospital in Winnipeg, after approximately twelve hours of labor. She weighed in at eight pounds. We were pleased to be blessed with a boy and a girl so we did not have to wish for a missing gender. With Alisha's arrival, we felt that our family was complete. We were certainly not aspiring to compete with the reproductive capabilities of our parents, who had nine children each in their respective families. Grace became a devoted full-time mother for Jeff and Alisha, while I focused on my career development.

During the three years before Alisha's arrival, I was bonding with Jeff, teaching him boys' stuff. Then Alisha come into my life and tugged at my heartstrings in a different way. Even before she was born, Jeff became her protective big brother: he told Dr. Waller, who was examining Grace during her last month of pregnancy with Alisha, that it was time for him to get the baby out of his mommy's tummy.

I felt a sense of added responsibility to isolate and protect this little angel from the experiences of my mother and sisters. In planning her protection, I made silent vows (some not so legal) to do the things I could not do to defend my mother and sisters from the abuses they endured in their marriages. Protecting my baby girl from abuse would also help me minimize the guilt I carried for my inability to stop the domestic violence that the women in my family endured.

In her early years, although Alisha was Daddy's girl, she really belonged to Mommy, to whom she ran for comfort whenever "the sky fell on her head." She was passionate about birthdays, birthday cakes, and presents—a passion she carried into her adulthood. Her individuality, not her gender, dictated how we raised her. She showed early signs of independence with a take-charge attitude that in a way taught us how to parent her. We were sure that as a teenager, she was going to be a hippie. She became a vegetarian, did not use makeup, and did not wear designer clothes because she felt comfortable in her own skin. She was real.

Watching her doting on her own two daughters, Lucy and Asha, brings back fond memories of her pretending to be the mom of her stuffed toys.

Chapter 12: My Career Path

The decision to delay our gratification for another year paid off in all the subsequent lucrative employment positions I was able to hold.

Royal Bank of Canada

In the spring of 1974, several employers held their annual job fair on the University of Manitoba campus, and from the offers I received, I chose a job with the Royal Bank of Canada as an assistant branch administrative officer at its Portage Avenue and Good Street branch in Winnipeg.

I was the first Trinidadian and the first visible minority to be seen on the other side of a bank's counter in Manitoba. Canadians were willing to judge me on my merit and not on my race, color, and, least of all, my family background. I felt I had finally gained the acceptance I had craved for so long. The trust I had placed in education as my passport to cross society's borders to upward mobility was finally paying dividends. I had made the transition from an invisible minority of no standing in my homeland to a visible minority being appreciated in my adopted country. In retrospect, I think I might have subconsciously chosen banking as my first career to compensate for the denied entry to banking in Trinidad, which, with few exceptions, was the preserve of the entrenched elites.

After a few months of training, I was promoted to branch administrative officer for the Morden, Manitoba, branch of the Royal Bank of Canada. Morden, at that time, was a Mennonite town with a population of just five thousand. The town is situated eighty-five miles south of Winnipeg, near the US border. It was a farming community famous for its corn and apple summer festival. I had gotten used to living the city life in Winnipeg and found Morden to be too slow-paced. Indra, Grace's youngest sister from Trinidad, moved in with us to attend school.

We lived there for about a year, during which time I learned to ice-skate on the local ice rink with Jeff, who was then four years old. Morden was so small that every time I fell in the skating rink on weekends, I would have the bank's customers describing my falls as they conducted their financial business at the bank during the week.

Public Service Commission

A job with the Saskatchewan government in Regina for a classification and pay research officer was advertised in the national newspapers. I applied for it and was flown to Regina for an interview. I was pleased that, out of dozens of applicants from throughout Canada, I was the successful applicant. The job paid significantly more than I was earning at the Royal Bank. I gave the bank the option to match the salary, but they could not because of pay-grade restrictions. We called in the movers and headed out through the prairies on the Trans Canada Highway to Regina, Saskatchewan, a six-hour drive.

Indra also moved with us to Regina and stayed for two more years before going to Chicago to continue her studies. For seven of the ten years that Grace and I spent in Canada, we enjoyed sharing our personal space with relatives in their formative years.

The Saskatchewan Public Service Commission (PSC) was responsible for classifying the jobs of fourteen thousand employees throughout the province who were entitled to appeal their job classifications. They were backed by their unions, which represented them in the appeals process. I successfully defended all my classification decisions before joint councils of labor and the PSC and was promoted to the position of pay research officer based on my performance.

We have fond memories of Regina and the friends we made there. Our neighbors were genuinely friendly folks. They all pitched in and helped me pave my driveway with concrete, and when we were away in the winters, they shoveled the snow for us. Gary Treble and his late wife, Noreen, remained the closest over the years.

Philip Morris International

In 1977 we spent our Christmas vacation in Trinidad, where I met Norberto Morinego, a Paraguayan gentleman, and his wife, who were tenants in one of Grace's parents' rental homes. He was the general manager for Philip Morris International at its Trinidad Licensee. He was being transferred to another country and thought that I was ideally qualified to replace him in Trinidad. My first reaction was that there was no way I would return to live in the country that had brought me so much emotional pain. He said he was sure that Philip Morris International would make me an offer that I could not refuse. He insisted that I send him my resume and said, "You could always refuse an offer, but at least know what you are refusing." That made sense to me, so I sent him my resume.

Six months later, when I had almost forgotten about our conversation, I received a call from John Behan, personnel director of Philip Morris International in New York. He said that if I was still interested in the position in Trinidad, I needed to go for a personal interview, on an all-expenses-paid trip, to their world headquarters at 100 Park Avenue, New York. The free trip to New York, where I had never been before, sounded more exciting than the thought of returning to Trinidad after ten years in Canada. So I went to New York City.

Philip Morris International was a division of Philip Morris USA Inc. (PM USA), which was the largest consumer-products conglomerate in the world. The company owned many cigarette brands, including Marlboro, the number one selling cigarette in the world. PM USA in 1980 was a holding company for several other companies, including Miller Brewing, Seven Up, Kraft, American Wine Growers, and Mission Viejo, a housing development company. Their brands were present in over two hundred countries. Their operating revenues of US$9.8 billion in 1980 was greater than the GDP of many countries, including Trinidad and Tobago, whose GDP in 1980 was US$5.75 billion.

The exclusivity and elegance of the Trump International Hotel and Towers, where I stayed, and the world headquarters of Philip Morris International at 100 Park Avenue, New York, were surreal experiences. Mental images of "the world headquarters for Doubles"—the Doubles Kitchen—clashed with the world headquarters of Philip Morris International and created trepidations of momentary doubt in myself.

I had interviews with John Behan, the director of Human Resources, and separately with four vice presidents from different areas of responsibilities. They were all very professional and affable officials. When the interviewing process was over, I left the world headquarters sensing that they would make me an offer, which I felt certain I was going to refuse. My anticipated refusal of any offer was not because of any antismoking sentiments I had as a nonsmoker, but because of the residual anxiety about rejection that persisted in my psyche when I thought of returning to Trinidad.

At that time, smoking tobacco products was fashionable, and marketing cigarettes in the highly competitive global markets was a lucrative pursuit. The US antismoking campaign wouldn't gain momentum and affect sales in the US domestic cigarette market until several years later. The international markets were, and still are, slow in adopting antismoking regulations.

Shortly after returning from New York, I received a written offer of employment for the position in Trinidad. The compensation package included all my moving expenses from Regina to Port of Spain, paid housing, automobile, private schooling for the children, entertainment expenses, medical benefits, and an annual home leave back to Canada. (It felt ironic that Philip Morris would employ me as a Canadian in my native country of Trinidad.) They also guaranteed the sale of our house in Regina at market value.

This was indeed an offer I could not and did not refuse. I thought that if the number one multinational corporation in the world at the time could have confidence in me to run their operations in Trinidad, then I was in a position to overcome any social hurdles that might still exist there. We moved back to Trinidad in November 1978— ten years and two children after Grace and I had first left for Canada—to assume my new responsibilities as Philip Morris International's general manager for its Trinidad Licensee operation.

I reported directly to Mr. Jose Pepe de la Torriente, the vice president of Latin America Area IV Division, which was responsible for duty-free and export sales to the Caribbean and Latin America. Area IV's offices, which included the Operations Division, were based in Miami, Florida. Everyone in those offices spoke Spanish as their primary language and English as a second language. Luckily, I had an aptitude for Spanish from high school in Trinidad, which I'd followed up with two courses at UM in Winnipeg. So all I had to do was brush up on the vocabulary of the new business in which I was now involved.

We stayed at the Trinidad Hilton for about three months until we cleared our personal effects from customs and found proper housing. When I was courting Grace, I would take her to the poolside bar of this upscale hotel for a nonalcoholic drink called a Bentley, and we often wondered what it would be like to be guests at this fine hotel. The staff at the Hilton treated us as foreigners because they were not used to seeing local Indians on an extended stay at the most expensive hotel in the country. Our hotel stay facilitated our transition back to life in Trinidad after ten years in Canada. The hotel staff treated us like family; they even prepared Jeff's school lunches when he started to attend Don Ross Elementary School from the hotel.

When I described my new job with all its benefits to my father, although he was extremely proud of my accomplishments, he asked me the most profound question, one that would take me over a decade to fully appreciate. He asked: "So you working for someone else? You not your own boss?" The job satisfaction and real power that he enjoyed in being his own boss in a business he created was worth more to him than any position that reports to a corporate boss. He was hinting to me that the creative freedom of an entrepreneur was more spiritually satisfying than the materialistic pursuit of a bureaucratic job. For an unlettered man, his common sense was so profound.

I went to my alma mater to report to Mr. Wilson on my academic and corporate achievements and to present him with the gift of a golden Cross pen set. I was saddened to learn that he had passed away a month before.

From the Hilton Hotel, we moved into a beautiful rental house in Glencoe, on the hills overlooking Bayshore and the Gulf of Paria and, on the horizon, the hills of San Fernando. It was a magnificent property that had a long driveway that ended at the semicircular front steps with a traffic circle, or a roundabout, in front of the house. The property was appropriately called "the Orchards" for its many fruit-bearing trees, mostly Julie mangoes and avocados.

We lived on this property for a few months until Grace's father had completed a beautiful house that I helped design from Canadian plans. It was located in the exclusive area of Regents Park, near the sea, south of Westmoorings. We leased this house from him for the duration of our stay in Trinidad.

My progress in Canada for ten years had been based on my merit, and now the number one American multi-national corporation had vetted me as qualified to run one of their international operations, so I was filled with confidence to return to Trinidad and break down any social barriers that might still exist. I was naïve. The colonial mentality was well preserved. The entrenched elites felt entitled by descent and perceived themselves as superior to the descendants of slaves and indentured laborers, regardless of how academically qualified the descendants were. The Licensee, distributor, and advertising agency were owned by the privileged local white elites, who were "whiter" than the broad-minded white people I interacted with in Canada and the United States.

Before Philip Morris International had entered Trinidad, the Licensee was on the verge of collapse. All the marketing and sales strategies were planned by Philip Morris's general manager, with some local input from the Licensee and its advertising agency, and presented to the vice president in Miami for approval. So in effect, the owner of the Licensee was taking directions from the Philip Morris GM until I arrived on the scene. He started to resist my directions and during a heated exchange said, "I do not take directions from cane cutters."

In the eyes of this neocolonialist Licensee owner, no academic qualification could supersede the qualification of one's status at birth. To him my ancestral status was my single identity; I was not supposed to rise above my circumstances. I couldn't believe I had to deal with this social prison that I thought I had escaped through education.

When Trinidad experienced an outbreak of typhoid, a local newspaper cautioned the population against eating street foods. The Licensee owner came into my office and, with his elitist gaze, said he'd read in the newspaper that my family was spreading typhoid with their Doubles. I was flabbergasted because I did not know that he knew I was the son of a Doublesman. It was a low blow. I had never brought up the subject of Deen's Doubles with him because there was no need, and in my corporate position, I was representing Philip Morris International, not Deen's Doubles. He had found out about my relation to Deen's Doubles from one of his employees who lived near my parents and had seen my car parked in front of their home, and he made the connection from my name.

At the end of a Marlboro Open Tennis Tournament that attracted world-renowned players such as Manuel Santana, Illie Nastase, Adriano Panatta, and others, I was the conspicuous official managing the event and making presentations to the winners. We had a grand dinner party at the Hilton Hotel ballroom with the international players and other invited guests. I was signing the dinner bill, which amounted to several thousands of Trinidad dollars, in the presence of the Licensee owner and his distributor—another privileged elite. The distributor, noticing the novelty of having a "cane cutter"

officiating in this white man's sport, asked me a most reveal-
ing question. He asked how I managed to get such a prestigious job. I sensed the inference of his question and retorted
that it was certainly not by the color of my skin.

Philip Morris International, through the Licensee, had
launched two brands of cigarettes in Trinidad before I arrived.
I managed the launch of the third brand. None of the three
brands were successful in capturing a significant share of the
market—for several key reasons. First, the main cigarette
manufacturer on the island was producing cigarettes from a
pure Virginia tobacco, while the Philip Morris brands used
US blended tobacco. The Trinidadian smokers were resistant
to change their smoking habit even for Marlboro, the number one selling cigarette in the world. The conversion of these
smokers would have been a long-term endeavor.

The second main reason was that Philip Morris International relied on the Licensee and its advertising agency for
their input into the local marketing strategy. At that time, all
radio, newspaper, billboard, and TV advertisements focused
on the middle-class African segment of the population as the
target market. The prevailing stereotype of Indians as penny-
pinching misers reinforced the advertising strategies. There
was a social agenda to marginalize Indians. Corporate adver-
tisers, through their controlled mass media, mastered and
professionalized the art of such cultural manipulation. As a
result, if there were any Indians in an advertisement, it would
be an Indian female with an African male. Or, in the case
of a television advertisement by the national airline BWIA,
the pilot was white, the stewardesses were white and French
Creoles, the ticketing agents were people of mixed races, and

the only Indian represented in the commercial was a baggage handler. Time has proven that this ill-conceived, distasteful, and flawed social engineering experiment using subliminal advertising was destined to fail.

When I raised the subject with the advertising agency that Indians made up over 40 percent of the total market and to make them invisible in an Afro-centric marketing strategy was to place our brands at a major disadvantage by not appealing to the entire cigarette market, their response was even more prejudiced, myopic, and socially divisive. They said that traditionally, products were not marketed to the Indian consumer and that if they were, the image of the product would be compromised. My illiterate father, who sold his Doubles to humans first, not Indians or Africans, could have taught these "literate" advertising professionals a lesson or two about marketing in a plural society. After forty-three years, he had succeeded in converting a nation's palette in making Doubles the number one street food in the country by using only word-of-mouth advertising to promote his product. For the promotion of Doubles, the Trini mouth had proven to be more effective than any subliminal advertising in the mass media!

It would take about thirty years for these marketing manipulators to realize that the Indian consumers were a lucrative market that their advertising campaigns should have been targeting. Nowadays, even international chain restaurants are successfully targeting the Indian-dominated areas of Trinidad, where the Indian consumers have destroyed the racist stereotype of the past.

Fierce competition from the de facto monopoly, a flawed and racist advertising campaign, and the consumers' resistance to change resulted in the failure of our third brand. I was faced with two options. I could recommend that we stay the course and invest in an uncertain long term, incurring annual losses in the millions of dollars, or cut our losses and close down the Licensee. However, terminating the Licensee would put my job on the line: I had no guarantee of a transfer since I was employed specifically for Philip Morris's Trinidad operation. Faced with this dilemma, I knew what option I had to choose.

I gambled with my job and recommended the termination of the Licensee. I was determined never to feel like a victim again and refused to listen to people saying or even thinking that I did not belong or I could not compete with the best in my field. To paraphrase Dr. Ben Carson, the person who has the most to do with me is me—not society or environment and certainly not someone else.

My gamble with my job paid huge dividends. My vice president, Mr. Jose de la Torriente, chose to make me the export sales manager for the Caribbean and Central America, based in Miami, Florida. The position had five sales representatives reporting to me in an area that accounted for annual sales in excess of US$50 million. Mr. de la Torriente's decision to include me on his executive team positively changed the course of my life.

Miami also offered the ideal compromise between my two worlds of Trinidad and Canada. My family and I could enjoy the tropical lifestyle that we longed for during the cold Canadian winters in Winnipeg and yet have the efficiencies of the Canadian system that we missed in Trinidad.

Twelve years after I first left Trinidad, I felt a sense of déjà vu—I was leaving again in search of a positive environment to maximize my potential. I understood then that my success would require more than my talent. It would require being surrounded by progressive-thinking people to bring out the best in me. I craved acceptance. I was certain that in the United States, as in Canada, my merit would be valued before my heritage, and my success would be almost guaranteed once I applied myself.

For me it seemed like history was repeating itself after 135 years. Many of the Indian indentured laborers who left India because of their ascribed low position in the traditional caste hierarchy found foreign lands offered better social mobility. When some returned to India at the end of their work contracts, they found the resettling very difficult. They had lost family and friends, who for religious and/or superstitious reasons, regarded them as polluted for crossing the *kala pani*, the black waters of the ocean. As a result, many re-indentured themselves and returned to settle in the countries of their original indentureship or in other British Commonwealth countries.

How similar I found my experience. I left Trinidad for better social mobility; I returned to find it difficult to resettle because of entrenched bigotry by persons who Joseph Campbell described as "Threshold Guardians" of the elite enclave. By returning to North America, I had refused to have my human spirit imprisoned by the cultural and institutional confines of Trinidad and Tobago. In America I could easily chart my destiny without the stifling social pressures I experienced in Trinidad attempting to bridge the social-class and racial divide. I felt that emigrating to North America would offer me and my young family a life of least resistance, one in which, to paraphrase Maya Angelou, I would become the dream and hope that my indentured ancestors fantasized about on their fateful journey across the *kala pani* all those years ago.

My nostalgic heartstring, like my "navel string," remains attached to the geography of my origins, which Robert Ardrey calls my "territorial imperative," and will never be snipped. You may take me out of Trinidad, but you cannot take Trinidad out of me, for I have tasted the *cascadoux* (a local fish that, myth says, once you eat, you will never leave Trinidad)!

My professional and entrepreneurial skills, knowledge, and experience give me a better opportunity to make a more effective contribution to Trinidad and Tobago from the United States of America, where I feel like a global citizen transcending geographical boundaries, race, ethnicity, religion, and class.

Modern communication technology now connects me more easily to my homeland than ever before and makes the cultural bonds stronger. The easy access to all the local news and current events of Trinidad and Tobago with streaming radio and TV programs on the Internet allow me to join the national dialog through blogs in the local online newspapers, e-mails, phone calls, and videoconferencing.

An important benefit of living in the United States, the world's hyperpower, is that it is a magnet for the world's best and brightest. The USA understands that to remain globally dominant, it must attract the most valuable human capital the world has to offer in terms of creativity, intelligence, and drive. Trinidad and Tobago benefits indirectly when some of its daughters and sons are located on the cutting edge of the world's human-capital frontier.

My new position as export sales manager with Philip Morris International gave me the opportunity to get first-hand knowledge of all the islands of the Caribbean, from Bermuda to Trinidad; Central America; and many countries in South America, including Venezuela, French Guyana, Suriname, Brazil, and Argentina. It was gratifying to go on a few business trips to some of these markets on Philip Morris's corporate jets, accompanied by senior executives, but in the case of Trinidad, to do so was sweet revenge for a "cane cutter" and son of the Doublesman.

Annual sales and marketing conferences were held in different countries each year, and that required some of my marketing presentations to be made in Spanish. These travels and conferences gave me the opportunity to appreciate differences in customs, culture, and business in such countries as Spain, Portugal, England, Italy, Brazil, Argentina, Mexico, and Venezuela, among others. The perks of this job included first-class travel and accommodations in top hotels at all my destinations, including the Waldorf Astoria Hotel in New York, where royalty and world elites often stayed. It was the zenith of affluence that a son of the Doublesman could have ever imagined. From being a waiter at the Fort Garry Hotel in Winnipeg, Manitoba, Canada, to being a guest at the Waldorf Astoria Hotel was an enjoyable reversal of roles.

When exotic trips to tourist destinations like Bermuda, the Bahamas, and other Caribbean islands became routine work, their allure diminished. The 50 percent travel schedule of the job made coming home a vacation. Luckily, Grace took charge of our home and the children when I was basically a part-time husband and father.

Nestlé

My employment with Philip Morris ended after ten years when the Miami offices were closed. I was given the option to be transferred to Singapore or to take a generous severance with full benefits for a year. I chose the latter and immediately found employment with the food giant Nestlé as a business manager in the Caribbean area, based in Miami. I was chosen for the position from a field of over seven hundred applicants. Most of Nestlé's distributors in the Caribbean were the same distributors for Philip Morris International, so it was more like a change of products than a change of company. After two years, Nestlé also had a major reorganization and downsized the Miami office. The export function was transferred to their Trinidad operation, and several positions, including mine, were eliminated. For obvious reasons, I did not consider asking for a transfer to Trinidad.

Caritrade, Inc.

My father's desire to chart his own destiny and be his own boss finally started to resonate with me. I activated my company, Caritrade, Inc., which I had incorporated in the state of Florida in 1985 as a contingency strategy. My education and experience in international business made me recognize what a great entrepreneurial pioneer my illiterate father was. His common sense was indeed made before books.

My excellent customer relations, which I developed over the dozen years with Philip Morris and Nestlé in the Caribbean, facilitated Caritrade's entry into the export business to these markets.

It is interesting that of all the products I could have exported through Caritrade, Inc., I gravitated to food products; even the bulk industrial products are for the food industry. Supplying food to consumers seems to be a genetic trait of mine.

The most interesting product that Caritrade, Inc., exported to Trinidad was bulk chickpeas—yes, chana. Through research I found out that Canada was producing a small-grain chickpea that, when soaked and cooked, had a 100 percent expansion ratio equivalent to the size of the more expensive larger-grain chickpeas.

With my firsthand knowledge of the Doubles business, I knew that this new small grain would work in the Doubles industry. The price was less than half that of the larger chickpeas, which would be a tremendous cost savings for the Doubles vendors. I approached one of the big importers of chickpeas with the proposal to change the type of chickpeas the Doubles vendors were using, but he resisted the concept. He categorically stated that Doubles vendors would not buy the small-grain chana.

I then proceeded to convince my brother Shamal to get involved with the importation of this type of chickpea. We called our private label Fairfield Foods to acknowledge the village of Fairfield's influence with the origin of Doubles. I shipped him several hundred tons of the new chickpeas, and Doubles vendors started to accept them once they saw the economic benefit of changing. Soon the big importers with deeper pockets caught on and flooded the market with small-grain chana, which they now classify as "Doubles chana." Fairfield Foods could not compete with the big importers, who had the resources to import larger quantities and warehouse and distribute nationally and, with their advantage of economies of scale, were able to undercut our pricing. We, however, succeeded in implementing a significant change in the Doubles industry to which we still feel so connected.

Even though I did not sell Doubles to earn a living like my father, his desire to have all of his sons involved in the Doubles business was fulfilled in my case when I sold hundreds of tons of chana through my export business. In fact, volume-wise, I sold more chana than my father sold in his forty-three years of promoting Deen's Doubles.

Caritrade, Inc., in addition to supplying innovative consumer and industrial products to my homeland, also gave me an opportunity to make a special contribution to Trinidad and Tobago. I was in the right place at the right time possibly to help save the life of President A. N. R. Robinson when he underwent a life-threatening surgery at the Eric Williams Medical Complex. Dr. Kamal Rampersad urgently needed a tracheotomy kit for the president, which I secured in Miami and placed on the next flight to Trinidad, and within hours the president was breathing through it.

Chapter 13: Jeff and Alisha

Grace and I had fully internalized the importance of education and imparted this cherished value to our two children, who luckily did not resist our influence. They were both model students who excelled in their respective academic fields.

Jeff is an attorney who married Padma, a vice president of Information Technology at City National Bank in Miami. They have given us two precious grandchildren, Gitanjali and Ameet.

Jeff won a full academic scholarship to Florida International University (FIU) for his undergraduate degree. Florida Governor Lawton Charles appointed him the student regent on the Florida State Universities Board of Regents. In 1992 he was the only collegiate debater in the United States to tie the British National Debate Team that defeated Yale, Princeton, Syracuse, and Cornell. In 1993 he was the only candidate from FIU nominated to compete for the Rhodes scholarship. He graduated magna cum laude, earning him a place among the top forty university students in the United States in *USA Today*'s annual salute to "America's best and brightest" in 1994.

At age twenty-one he took an academic hiatus for a year to teach speech and debate at Braddock Senior High School in Miami, where he told his students he was twenty-three years old and grew a mustache to look older than the physically bigger students he was teaching.

Before starting law school at Florida State University in Gainesville, he went to London, England, and Benares, India, to study Indian classical tabla (Indian drums) under the tutelage of his guru, the world-renowned tabla maestro Pandit Sharda Sahai. The Benares *gharana* (or style) of tabla playing, which is formally taught at the Banaras Hindu University, was created by the Sahai family in Benares, India, and Pandit Sharda Sahai was the living heir in the family's tabla lineage. On that trip, Jeff met his future wife, Padma, the daughter of his guru.

He continued to excel academically at the University of Florida's College of Law and graduated cum laude in the top 6 percent of his class. His many awards and honors include: Order of the Coif, Order of the Barristers, Best Oralist on the Moot Court Team in 1997, Best Advocate in the "Final Four" Trial Team of 1997, and Honors in Legal Research and Writing.

Upon graduating from law school, he was chosen to do his internship under the Honorable Chief Judge Robert Mark of the US Bankruptcy Court Southern District of Florida, one of the most prestigious internships for law graduates. After this internship he was called to the bar and started to work for the top bankruptcy law firm in Miami—Belzin, Sumberg, Dunn Axelrod & Baena, LLP—where he stayed for a year before starting his own practice.

In 2001 he opened the Law Offices of Jeffrey Deen, P.A., in Miami, where he practiced consumer and commercial bankruptcy for a few years and has since been practicing residential and commercial real estate and title insurance. Being his own boss would have made his grandfather MamooDeen a very proud man.

Jeff's facility with the English language is remarkable and particularly pleasing to me, considering his generational proximity to a period of illiteracy when the best English that could have been spoken was "Hinglish."

Both Jeff and Alisha manifested the musical genes of my father. Alisha is an accomplished flutist who teaches the techniques of the instrument in her spare time. Jeff was born to be a musician. In his toddler years, he was beating on pots and pans in the kitchen, and from the time he could stand up, he was swaying to the sound of reggae music played on our stereo. Later on he played the recorder, flute, and saxophone but gravitated to the drums. In high school he was in the drum line of the school marching band and was the drummer in his first band, which started in my garage.

Jeff founded Drumming for Wellness, Inc., and as a professional musician and drum circle facilitator/instructor, facilitates drumming events for corporate team-building, for empowerment of special-needs children to improve their cognition and motor skills, and for stress relief and meditation for adults. He is also creating and recording music that fuses the Indian tabla with other world instruments. Video clips of him playing the tabla and other percussion instruments, such as the *hapi* and *hang* drum, are on YouTube under "Jeff Deen."

An interesting chain of events in my family's history revolves around passion: My father turned his back on the agrarian lifestyle with a passionate dream to be his "own boss." I rejected my father's business with a passion for education and the corporate executive lifestyle. Now Jeff is turning away from his law practice to follow his passion for music and spirituality.

Jeff spiritually understands true power. He no longer craves wealth and position and is less attached to possessions. He has rejected being dominated by great ambition or enslaved by his desires. He thinks more clearly as he voluntarily chooses simplicity.

Alisha is married to Dr. Jason Steindler, an anesthesiologist and a pain management specialist. They added two more jewels to our grandparents' crown named Lucy Kaveri and Asha Grace.

Alisha is an alumnus of Florida International University and the University of Oregon, where she received her BA and MS, respectively, in environmental studies. For her MS at Oregon, she explored the gap between environmental outreach efforts and immigrant communities of color in her ethnographical graduate thesis, titled "Conservation as an Indo-Caribbean Cultural Value: Immigration, Globalization, and Multicultural Environmental Education in South Florida."

Her focus on environmental justice in water-management policies started with a federal task force for ecosystem restoration in South Florida. During her undergraduate years at FIU, she was already out protesting the negative impact of sugar production on the Florida Everglades. Her placard read, "How Sweet It's Not." We were always worried that she would be handcuffed and thrown in jail for being an environmental activist; she was disappointed that she was never arrested for her activism.

Alisha's early passion for the environment has led her to a career as an environmentalist. For academic and career reasons, she and her husband, Jason, have resided in South Florida; Eugene, Oregon; San Francisco; Philadelphia; Michigan; and Albany, New York. In each place she found her environmental advocacy niche.

She fought for inclusion and equity for people of color and immigrant communities in environmental policies in both the Detroit area and the San Francisco Bay Area. In California, she advocated for these communities at the state legislature in Sacramento. With her colleagues at Clean Water Action/Clean Water Fund (San Francisco), United Farm Workers, and Latino Issues Forum, her policy advocacy succeeded in getting the California Department of Health Services to set aside $100 million for disadvantaged communities for drinking-water projects. She made a significant contribution toward institutionalizing environmental justice into water policy when she presented "Thirsty for Justice" at the California Water Board Annual Conference in 2005.

In Philadelphia and Allentown, she focused not only on water-policy issues but on air quality as well, and got a small community organization in South Philadelphia to sue successfully the Sunoco Refinery for air-quality violations. The settlement funds were used to purchase some real-time air-monitoring equipment that South Philadelphians continue to use to catch air-quality violations. In Southeastern

Pennsylvania townships, she and her staff changed local municipal ordinances to increase water protection in six different townships surrounding Philadelphia.

Alisha is living a life that my mother and three sisters could not have even imagined. The cultural norms of their impoverished lives in male-dominated households that were full of children denied them formal education and dictated that pot spoons were mightier than pens for their survival. The cultural norms did not allow them to aspire, as Alisha did, to an independent lifestyle that could have a positive effect on society, but rather to cowering servility that stifled their full human potential to lead self-determined lives.

Chapter 14: MamooDeen's Legacy

The move back to Trinidad gave me the opportunity to reconnect with my parents and to spend the last four months of my father's life in close proximity to him. On March 13, 1979, at age sixty-two, Papa passed away from congestive heart failure while resting on his bunk bed in the Doubles Kitchen. When I got the news, I was told he was very sick and I should come right away. Not knowing that he had already died, I went looking for a cardiologist friend, who was playing tennis at the Hilton Hotel, to make arrangement for Papa to see him. When I finally arrived at my parents' home, I saw Grace's parents and many other people gathered at the house. I knew then that we had lost Papa.

The news of his death spread rapidly to his many relatives and friends throughout the island. Edool and Shamal from Winnipeg and Sharm and Alick from Sudbury took the first available flights from Canada to attend the funeral.

Ma once again entered the abyss of her darkest emotions, which, though familiar by now, did not lessen the pain of another loss. Despite the vicissitudes of her marriage, MamooDeen, her life and business partner of forty-three years, protected her. Even though he was survived by seven of their children, she now felt alone.

Papa's body was brought to the house and placed in front of his Doubles Kitchen for the final viewing. The house, yard, and road in front of the house were packed with people. Sharm recalls that Hamidan, who was in denial of losing our Papa, touched the body and raised one of his eyelids momentarily, as if to make certain that what she was experiencing was real. Ma was the last to see Papa's face during the viewing ceremony. With her three daughters close to her, Ma, in bidding her last farewell to her now-silent partner, said, "OK, go now; the boys are waiting for you" (referring to Habil and Cabil). She then took one end of the cotton shroud that wrapped the body and covered his face.

The funeral procession left the house for the El Socorro Muslim cemetery, where he was buried in an unmarked grave. For the Islamic burial ceremony, Papa's body, wrapped in a white cotton shroud, was placed in the grave without a coffin. The two men who volunteered to go into the grave to receive the body were Choate's son Anwar and Papa's first son Hollis, our half brother. Grace refused to stay at home with the other women, as was the custom, and chose instead to give me the support I needed at the cemetery.

Papa's Life: A Story of Possibility

MamooDeen was born in a house facing a mountain of the Central Range in Piparo and died in a house facing a mountain of the Northern Range in Santa Cruz, neither of which he had ever climbed. But the mountain of struggles in his life that he successfully ascended kept his family together and out of abject poverty. In defiance of an oppressive system, this illiterate peasant pulled himself up by the bootstraps, charted a different destiny, and achieved his life's goal of being his own boss in a business he manifested from a simple idea.

His life is a story of possibility. He did not wait for the state to guide or lift him up toward entrepreneurship. He was determined to succeed despite the state, rather than because of it. His confidence came not from believing that he was inferior or by associating his plight with his birth, but by his indomitable will and strong belief that the world of his dreams was possible. This motivated him to answer desperation with ingenuity and spend his life in pursuit of conquering the abject poverty and servility that colonialism inflicted on him and his people.

He had kept his promise that illiteracy would not deter him from using his common sense and physical strength to support and protect his family. He left Ma, his lifetime business partner, financially secure, so she did not have to cook any more Doubles when he was gone. I am using my financial inheritance from his estate to finance the self-publishing of this book; so in effect he even paid for the cost of telling his own story. This was the measure of the man endearingly named MamooDeen.

He did not capitalize on the Doubles industry that he created. His illiteracy might have denied him the knowledge of patents, trademark rights, franchising, and royalties that could have made him a materially wealthy man. But intellectual property rights were not protected in those days in Trinidad.

He has, however, joined an exceptional group of other entrepreneurs and pioneers in the world who did not capitalize on their creations. Among the many is Daisuke Inoue, famous for inventing the first karaoke machine and losing out on roughly $110 million in royalties by not patenting it. The pioneering doctors Jean and Alastair Carruthers never got to cash in on their discovery of Botox as an anti-aging treatment because they never patented their own discovery. Shepherd-Barron, creator of the automated teller machine (ATM), one of the best and most widely used inventions of the modern era, refused to patent the idea and spent the remainder of his life an average Joe. George Crum, the man who made the first batch of potato chips, didn't have the political power to maximize his profits from his own creation. He was both African American and Native American and lived from 1822 to 1914. "In those days, people of color were not allowed to take out patents on their inventions," says Gant-Britton, author of the textbook *Holt African American History.* And Walter Diemer, who invented bubble gum, which became the most successful one-cent treat on the candy market, neglected to patent his invention.

MamooDeen's mission in life was not motivated by maximizing profit but charitably driven to feed poor people like himself with a low-cost, high-protein, nutritious, vegan street food that was within their meager means. He selflessly taught the trade to his relatives, friends, and strangers alike who were experiencing the same vicious cycle of poverty as he did. Instead of throwing away the left-over chutney from his daily Doubles inventory, he would give it to any nearby competing Doublesman in San Juan. In his altruism, he was

like the proverbial candle that did not lose its glow by light-
ing other candles. He was like a warrior gathering his troops
to fight the common enemies named poverty and exploitation. His mission was to spread the spirit of entrepreneurship
with his Doubles business, which for him represented a celebration of struggle and triumph over an oppressive system.

Doubles vendors started popping up and replicating
MamooDeen's business model in every town and village.
Some even aggressively placed their Doubles Boxes near to
his in direct competition with him in San Juan. Some Dou-
blesmen replicated his compartmentalized yellow Doubles
Boxes on freight bikes while others tried to differentiate their
imitation by painting their Doubles Boxes in different colors.
But the one thing they could not duplicate was the taste of
Deen's Doubles, because MamooDeen was an "eyeball cook."
He cooked by the senses of sight, smell, touch, taste, and
hearing. He cooked by instinct, not by measurement. With
his "tasty hand," he left a delicious legacy.

He had switched on an entrepreneurial engine of financial freedom and independence directly in Princes Town,
San Fernando, San Juan, and Port of Spain, and indirectly in
the rest of the nation. Even though only two of his six sons
followed his Doubles dream to fruition, he had succeeded in
motivating hundreds of nationals to follow in his footsteps.
Faced with high unemployment, they were inspired by his
business model to be self-employed and gain entrepreneurial independence. Among those who invested their energies
in the unforgiving Doubles business, several are rewarded
with significant wealth for their dedication and hard work.
They are living MamooDeen's dreams. He would be proud

to know that so many people, especially the families of his brothers-in-law, the Alis of Princes Town and San Fernando, have embraced his intelligent foresight and helped to make Doubles the number one street food of Trinidad and Tobago.

The fact that we now take the accomplishments of the Doubles business for granted underscores how significant its progress has been, given that seventy-seven years ago its success would have been considered unthinkable. These achievements depended on the sustained commitment and sacrifice of an extraordinary entrepreneur committed to a vision of his world. He gave his life to something bigger than himself. His achievements were the manifestation of his character. Trinidad at the time presented him with the ideal setting for his life's adventure.

When MamooDeen introduced Doubles in 1936, he was making his contribution to the blending of the Indian culture with a plural society in its infancy. The national buffet of culinary delights has been enriched by his creative input. His contribution to nation-building stirred the melting pot of a diverse society that now describes itself as "all ah we is one." Calypso icon David Rudder described Doubles on his Facebook page, in December 2012, as "the great egalitarianizer of all varied stomachs."

MamooDeen's untimely demise at age sixty-two denied him the opportunity to see his creation take flight to become the ubiquitous street food of the nation, but his immortality will reside in his creation that lives. He may have lived an uneducated and ordinary life, but he left an extraordinary legacy.

Although he has not been officially recognized for the national heritage he created for his country of birth, he has left "a personal check payable to Trinidad and Tobago for an amount in excess of his lifespan." As a rural rube with a vision, he was the ideal of a self-made man who came and gave without taking.

Jamaloo

Jamaloo Deen circa 1984

During the 1980s, Shamal would return, during the long Winnipeg winters, to Trinidad to help our brother Jamaloo in the Deen's Doubles operation. Shamal took charge of the production, while Jamaloo and Subrattan's son Balo controlled sales. Two of Hamidan's sons were brought on board: Moody in sales and Tasmool in production. With young blood, business started to increase rapidly. Seven outlets were established in the San Juan area to cater to the rising demand that was created. This was the period of highest sales in the history of Deen's Doubles.

The income generated from the increase in business allowed Jamaloo to buy the property next door that was previously owned by Mr. Ali and his wife, Kala. He demolished the building and built an impressive two-story house, which remains the high point of our family's material achievement in Trinidad. It is the house that Deen's Doubles built. Ma also had the security of having Jamaloo and his family living next door, since she slept alone in her empty nest when Shamal returned to Winnipeg for the summer months.

Jamaloo's house

What is even more remarkable about the property that Jamaloo bought next door was the sense of vindication we felt toward Mr. Ali, who had discouraged our brother-in-law Alick from joining our family because we were "low-class Doubles vendors."

Jamaloo went on to purchase other properties on Santa Cruz Old Road as investments. His material wealth was his reward for the sacrifice he made for thirty-three years, beginning at age fifteen, in the family business. Deen's Doubles gave Jamaloo the wherewithal to keep his family, especially his disabled son, David, financially secure. Shamal financed his Winnipeg restaurant operation from the income he earned in the joint venture with Jamaloo. The two sons of MamooDeen who stayed loyal to the business reaped the belated financial rewards of Deen's Doubles—and deservedly so.

Jamaloo was generous to a fault with his money. The more he made, the more he gave away. Most of his friends were Afro-Trinis who called him *Mamoo* (uncle). Some people took advantage of his generosity, but it never bothered him. He must have inherited this trait from Papa, who gave from the little he had.

As the Doubles business grew with his young team of Shamal, Balo, Moody, and Tasmool and generated significant disposable income, Jamaloo started to gamble at card games in some of the surrounding gambling clubs. His favorite card games were *All Fours* and *Wapi*. His ability to count money rapidly and to memorize several orders for Doubles simultaneously served him well in the card games that relied on memory and quick mental calculations. As a high roller, he won and lost large sums of money. Luckily, he played only with his disposable income.

I was on a business trip to Trinidad one time when Jamaloo complained about shortness of breath and severe pain and swelling in his hands and feet. I decided to bring him to Miami for medical treatment. In Trinidad, Charchie, an older lady who was a friend of our family's, had told him that someone had performed *obeah* on him, which caused the affliction. No one had disputed Charchie's diagnosis because superstitious beliefs in *obeah* were stronger than in science. So I took Jamaloo with me to the passport office and got his passport issued in one day. He came to Miami and received medical treatment for both his conditions.

The pain and swelling of his hands and feet were found to be gout, not *obeah,* of course, and the medicine prescribed quickly alleviated the discomfort.

His shortness of breath however, was the symptom of a much more insidious heart condition called alcohol cardiomyopathy in which the heart muscle becomes susceptible to alcohol and deteriorates even with small quantities of the substance. The end result is congestive heart failure. The cardiologist who saw him at the Cedars Heart Center in Miami was a Trinidadian named Dr. Ling. His prescription for survival was for Jamaloo to have a lifestyle change with respect to his diet, smoking, and alcohol consumption. Dr. Ling warned him against having even a little alcohol and asked him to start on an exercise program, beginning with walking.

A few years after his medical alert, Jamaloo became complacent and reverted to his old ways. On April 29, 1990, at the young age of forty-seven, he succumbed to his heart condition. He is survived by his wife, Nooran; two daughters, Ann and Melissa; and David, a special-needs son.

At his wake, villagers lit candles on the streets leading to his home and played African drums throughout the night. At dawn, some of us who got a few hours of sleep were awakened to the sound of slow drumbeats that were now a dirge for Jamaloo. The slow drumbeats synchronized with the beats of our heavy hearts and made us limp with emotion.

Jamaloo, like our father, had transcended race during his lifetime. The timid and quiet Indian boy from the village of Fairfield who at age fifteen had come to the north to peddle his father's product had won the hearts of the non-Indian community he fed with Deen's Doubles daily for thirty-three years. He even became friends with the "badjohns" of the Croisée, and they protected him. His wake, which was taken over by his Afro-Trini customers and friends, spoke volumes of his interpersonal relationship with the diverse population. He was embraced by all.

Nazimul "Balo" Ali

In 1972 when he was twelve years old, my nephew Balo had to leave his parents, Subrattan and Dood, in Ecclesville, Rio Claro, and move in with Ma and Papa to be nearer to his high school, Hillview College in Tunapuna. He was a very intelligent boy who had great love and respect for Ma and Papa, his grandparents, whom he called Nani and Nana. He excelled in high school and obtained his A-levels certification in 1979, which qualified him for the job market or university.

Having lived with Ma and Papa throughout his high school years, he also gained firsthand knowledge of the Doubles business. His part-time income was derived from helping in all aspects of the Doubles business. When he compared what the prevailing job market would pay for his qualifications versus an income from selling Doubles for his grandparents, he opted for the latter. He soon became the face of Deen's Doubles in the Croisée. His dexterity in wrapping Doubles at sixteen per minute made him the fastest Doublesman of his time.

He married Sandra, a beautiful niece of Alick's. They have three children: Stacy-Ann, Andre, and Nicholas. After Jamaloo's death in 1990, Balo launched his own brand of Doubles—Dee-Balo's (a hybridized name from Deen and Balo). Papa's employment mantra to "be your own boss" resonated with Balo. With hard work and determination, Balo and Sandra grew their business to two restaurants in Port of Spain. Balo is also involved in large-scale catering to all-inclusive carnival fetes and other major events where Doubles have become a staple on the menu.

Alick's parents' homestead, the landmark property of the Paguandas clan, situated obliquely opposite the La Venezuela statue at 23 Santa Cruz Old Road, went up for sale and Balo and Sandra bought it in 1994. The purchase kept the nostalgic address in the Paguandas family through Sandra, a granddaughter. In 1997 Balo and Sandra proceeded to build a mansion on the property with a modern dedicated Doubles Kitchen to produce DeeBalo's Doubles.

One of Balo's upper-middle-class neighbors was very concerned that he might build a Doubles Depot in front of his new house, which the neighbor believed would depreciate the value of the surrounding properties. The neighbor even offered to buy the front lot of the property to remove the anticipated "eyesore" that Doubles vending would create.

The old stereotypical image of the Doublesman as one who "begs for a living at the side of the road" still persists in the minds of some people.

Rasulan's Sunset Years

Ma was convinced that she was dealt a bad hand in the game of life. The angel of premature deaths seemed to enjoy our hospitality as he callously trampled on our broken hearts, like Hurricane Andrew ravaging my dream home and pristine surroundings in Miami. On her list of losses, Ma had the premature loss of her mother and father; her baby brother Cassim, whom she raised as her firstborn; three sons; her stepson Hollis; three grandchildren; and her husband. She envied them for having the luxury of death while she was still bound to a miserable world of mental anguish. She was left to see distorted images of her world through her remaining tears, which somehow still flowed to soothe her tired eyes. She felt ready to embrace the angel of death herself. For her, a place that was now the safe abode of so many of her loved ones must be far better than her earthly domain of despair, and she prayed for the mercy of death.

To distract her from her life of grievous solitude, we coaxed her into visiting her children and grandchildren in Miami, Toronto, and Winnipeg. On Ma's first trip to Miami, I had the pleasure of having her travel first class with me on Eastern Airlines. She reminded me that the modes of transportation in her life's journey were from bull-cart to Boeing, from rough dirt roads to traveling without roads.

The surviving children tried to keep her in the United States and Canada, but she preferred to live in her own home in Trinidad, where the memories of her dearly departed coexisted with her familiar surroundings. Papa and Ma created an independent lifestyle that did not make them dependent on the state or their children. When Ma was qualified to receive a government old-age pension, she refused to apply for it because in her self-made world, she believed it would be a failure and disgrace to be a ward of the state. In this respect, she felt much more elevated in a social system that marginalized her and her family.

Surviving siblings in 1997, left to right: Shamal, Hamidan, Sharm, Badru, Edool.

Ma insisted on living alone in her home until her loneliness became worse than her grief. We arranged for her to live with Hamidan and Waheed in Tableland, where the company of some of her grandchildren and great-grandchildren distracted her from ruminating on her life of loss.

Hamidan and Waheed, with their limited elementary education, also saw the value of education and steered three of their four children into white-collar jobs. Sally became a nursing instructor; Faresha and Moody are elementary schoolteachers. The second son, Tazmool, who was trained in MamooDeen's Doubles Kitchen in Santa Cruz Old Road, sells Doubles part time in Princes Town under his brand name, Taz. The taste of his Doubles is the nearest to Deen's Doubles because he was exposed to the recipe. When he is not selling Doubles, he pursues his agricultural interests.

On November 1, 1994, at age seventy-four, Ma passed away in dignity, surrounded by loved ones. Death to her was the final freedom for her tormented soul. The angel of death could punish her no more.

Her funeral procession from Tableland stopped in front of the Fairfield homestead property to underscore the significance of the location where seven of her nine children were born and where Deen's Doubles gained its recognition. She was buried in Navet Cemetery in Princes Town, a few feet away from where her Habil and Cabil had laid waiting for her for thirty-seven years.

The night of the funeral was *Diwali*, the Hindu festival of lights that symbolizes light over darkness. Homes were brightly lit with thousands of *diyas* (little oil lamps made from clay with cotton wicks dipped in vegetable oil or ghee). It was a fitting farewell symbol for the end of her life's dark journey to be in light in the vicinity of Fairfield, where she entered this world.

From the pursuit of her elusive happiness, she took with her the scars of her life's battles—a heart many times broken and eight fingers that were significantly curved upward from spreading the dough to make baras during the forty-three years that she produced Deen's Doubles.

Hurricane Andrew

On August 24, 1992, my material world was turned upside down by Hurricane Andrew, a category 5 storm that packed winds of over 165 miles per hour. We were located in the northern eye-wall of Andrew, which is the most destructive part of a hurricane. Since our house was located in the coastal area, we were subjected to mandatory evacuation.

After boarding up the house as best we could and securing most of our personal effects, Grace, Alisha, and I headed in the early evening of August 23, 1992, to Orlando with our cocker spaniel Coco and our important documents. With the devastating forecasts we were getting from the hurricane center and the threat of an eighteen-foot tidal wave, we understood that we must leave all material possessions behind and get out of harm's way to preserve our lives. We stayed with Grace's mother, who lived in Orlando at that time. Evacuation started early in the day, and even though the turnpike and I-95 were converted to one-ways heading north, the traffic was still a nightmare. Luckily, because of our late departure, the traffic situation had improved a little, and we arrived in Orlando six hours later—almost twice the normal travel time.

We were glued to the TV watching CNN's coverage of the impending disaster. When Andrew made landfall, we were certain our house and our vacation home in Key Largo would both sustain damage.

Considering the large population in Andrew's path, it was amazing that only forty people perished. More than 250,000 people became homeless; more than 80,000 businesses were destroyed. Unable to deal with the disaster, about 100,000 residents permanently left the South Dade County area in Andrew's wake. When damage assessments were made and reported in the local media, Andrew had caused $30 billion in property damage, which at the time was the costliest disaster in US history.

It seemed like nature had attacked itself with its impact on the environment. A significant amount of the coral reef at Biscayne National Park was destroyed, and most of South Dade's native pinelands, mangrove, and tropical hardwood hammocks were damaged. It was estimated that Andrew created thirty years worth of debris.

Our first attempt to return home the next day was aborted by the early curfew placed on the affected area and so we finally got to Miami two days later. There were no working street lights; citizens were directing traffic, and street signs were nonexistent. Power lines were strewn across streets covered by fallen trees and other debris; lamp poles were twisted and broken like matchsticks. It was interesting to discover how much we rely on landmarks for our bearings, because in their absence we were easily lost or disoriented.

The blackened tree trunks that remained standing were denuded of their branches and leaves and stood like wounded sentries on duty surveying the devastation of a war zone. My neighborhood was redolent of the ocean and sea life. The sounds of chainsaws and portable generators filled the air. These sounds indicated that the rebuilding of devastated lives had begun.

When Grace, Alisha, Coco, and I finally found our home, we were surprised that the building was still standing and looked intact from the outside. When we attempted to enter our home, however, we were traumatized. Our dream home was now a house of horrific nightmares.

Andrew had blown right through our home, taking most of our material possessions and dumping them in the waterway alongside the house. What Andrew could not take with it through the blown-out doors and windows was ransacked, as if the Incredible Hulk had fought a furious battle inside my house.

The eighteen-foot tidal wave that came ashore left four-foot watermarks inside our house where the water settled before receding. What was left of our destroyed possessions was mingled with dead fish and other marine life on the floor, one foot of mud, and sand from the ocean throughout the house and yard. This was the evidence left by Hurricane Andrew's flash flood that thrashed the coastal area. The inside of our house became one with nature. The only life-forms Andrew left on my property were the fish and shrimps that were still alive in our swimming pool, now filled with seawater. Ceiling fans were not made to rotate at 165 miles per hour; all the blades of all the ceiling fans in the house had disappeared.

The decision to obey the evacuation warnings certainly saved our lives, for had we stayed in the house, we could not have survived nature's fury. In surveying the devastation of our homestead, we had mixed emotions for the material losses but were simultaneously happy that our lives were spared so we could rebuild our home. We had two options: cry or pick up shovels. We did both.

The courage to start cleaning up the disaster and rebuilding required drawing from the deep recesses of my parents' feelings when they had faced adversity. I could have chosen to deal with the disaster like my mother and suffer in the pursuit of losses of which I had no control or rebuild my life like my father, who stared adversity in the eyes and said, "Is that all you got?" To crash and burn was my opportunity to learn what my father already understood—to get oneself up, dust off, and go at it again. By falling many times, he had not just observed life, he had lived life. My father's life was a living lesson on the resilience of the human mind, body, and spirit, and it taught me how to ride on the backs of adversity and loss to reach the finish line.

The first night of our return we cleaned out the master bathroom, where Grace, Alisha, and Coco slept on the floor. I tried sleeping in a car in the driveway. Once the decision was made to rebuild, we felt better remaining on location. It was a waste of time to find hotel accommodations, which would entail commuting back and forth through dangerous streets that were claiming lives in Andrew's wake. Chaos was the norm; price gouging for ice, gasoline, and generators was rampant; people were fighting for ice; and looting of businesses had started. The blue tarps on roofs brought back some color to the desolate landscape.

Royal Caribbean Cruises, where Grace was employed, was generous in providing temporary accommodations for affected employees and their families on their cruise ships at the port of Miami. Grace and Alisha stayed only one night on the cruise ship because the contrast between the luxury of the cruise ship and the now-primitive surroundings of our home gave them a feeling of confused guilt about leaving Coco and me in our muddy mess. They abandoned ship and returned to be a part of the cleanup operation and the rebuilding of our home.

Jeff, who was studying tabla in Toronto when Hurricane Andrew struck, coordinated his return trip with my brothers Edool and Shamal, who took the first flight out of Winnipeg, to come to our rescue. They flew into Orlando, borrowed Grace's sister Ruby's van, and loaded up cleaning supplies, tarps, tools, food, and other items that were in short supply in Miami. Grace, Alisha, and I greeted their arrival with a huge sigh of relief. We now had the manpower to tackle the cleanup operation in earnest. Shamal and Edool gave us the moral and physical support we so desperately needed to deal with the catastrophe of losing all of our material possessions. They were the two rays of light and hope in the darkest disaster in my life. They were like the reincarnations of Habil and Cabil when I truly needed my bhaiyas the most. Edool described our muddy mess as "mudness."

For about six weeks, there was no electricity or phones, and the water supply was minimal. We could only work in the daylight hours. We ate a lot of canned foods and cooked on a portable gas stove on the patio. We slept on wet mattresses covered with plastic sheets in the house with no doors and windows, flashlights strapped to our wrists.

When looting started in the residential areas, one of my neighbors lent me a shotgun for protection. It was the first time I had held a shotgun, and I still don't know if I would have been able to use it.

When the major cleanup of our house was completed in about a week, Shamal and Edool returned to their homes in Winnipeg.

Luckily, our insurance covered all of our losses. We bought a large mobile trailer, parked it on the driveway, and slept in it for six months as the house was being rebuilt. I assumed the role of a general contractor and subcontracted the different aspects of the reconstruction work to firms and individuals.

The year it took to rebuild the house was the most challenging year of our lives. Had it not been for the life of simplicity I had lived in Trinidad, I could not have led my family through this disaster. Tens of thousands of American families abandoned the area; many marriages were split apart under the stressful circumstances in Andrew's wake. We were determined to deal with the disaster and rebuild.

The Final Chapter of Deen's Doubles

Deen's Doubles Depot

Jamaloo's death meant that the history of Deen's Doubles was in its final chapter. Shamal's annual travels, spending winters in Trinidad and summers in Winnipeg, had taken a toll on his marriage, which ended after thirty years. His Deen's Restaurant was sold, and the new owner retained the Deen's name to capitalize on the goodwill that Shamal and his family had created for the business. Shamal returned to Trinidad permanently to upgrade and run the last outlet for Deen's Doubles in Trinidad: Deen's Doubles Depot, which he built in 1985 in front of the family's house on Santa Cruz Old Road, San Juan.

With Shamal's Midas touch, Deen's Doubles Depot rose again from the ashes to create a renewed demand for Deen's Doubles and rotis that he and his wife, Nuroon, are busily satisfying. Customers come from near and far, creating daily traffic jams on Santa Cruz Old Road. They appreciate the Canadian standards that he brought to Deen's Doubles Depot from his twenty-seven years of catering to Canadians in his Winnipeg restaurant.

Shamal's efforts and passion to keep Deen's Doubles alive despite the series of Deens' misfortunes is a tribute to the innovative and fresh thinking of our father, who, by example, taught us to get up when adversity strikes us down and always dream beyond our circumstances.

When Shamal closes the doors to this final sales outlet, it will bring to an end the saga of Deen's Doubles.

Son of a Doublesman

This memoir of the first family of Doubles should finally put to rest the factual inaccuracies of the origin of Doubles in

Trinidad and Tobago. MamooDeen's legacy is sustained only by the truth that was told by the many eyewitnesses whose recollections of the oral history are credible, reliable, and compelling.

My parents made no claims to greatness, and yet when I look back seventy-seven years, I marvel at what they accomplished, and I owe them recognition, respect, gratitude, and life. And in that spirit, I wrote this memoir.

The writing of this memoir has also been a cathartic exercise in embracing my formative background years and circumstances from which evolved the complex of characteristics that distinguishes me as an individual. It has taken me over five decades to navigate the painful insecurities from the shame I experienced in my impressionable years in Trinidad, where teenage bullying and society's devalued status of the Doublesman and his family played major roles in shaping my character.

My academic and professional life in Canada and the United States of America only helped me to live behind a mask of anonymity to conceal the imposed stigma of being a son of the Doublesman in Trinidad. But it did not conceal me from myself. I had to go back and rescue the little boy who was still whimpering with insecurities in that dark corner of his subconscious and was ashamed of his background. I had to accept who I am and recognize that I am perfect in my way and that it is safe to be me, to show up without apology for simply being myself. I had to remember the past that I tried so hard to forget and give up the false hope that it could be different. By excavating my long-buried authentic self and confronting my deep personal feelings of shame, I found redemption in the gift of true self-acceptance before becoming whole again.

The accomplishments of the first family of Doubles are not measured in academics, careers, or net worth, but in the journey that started in the Doubles Kitchen—a place that is now so far away and yet so close. They are measured in the psychological distances from the rural village of Fairfield, Princes Town, in Trinidad, to the University of Manitoba, Canada; from illiteracy to economics, marketing, law, medicine, science, and information technology in just two generations. They are measured from the Doubles Kitchen to the American dream, which James Truslow Adams describes as "a better, richer and fuller life for everyone, with opportunity for each according to ability or achievement regardless of social class or circumstances of birth."

My past certainly has influenced who I am, but I was ultimately responsible for the individual I became. My identity, which started as the son of a Doublesman and which I repressed for most of my life, has come full circle to remind me that this is the identity I must embrace to bring closure in accepting my reality. My upbringing was a blessing, not a curse. Beneath my biggest wounds of poverty, privation, early loss of loved ones, scant respect, and sadness, lies my greatest gift: a heart that knows deep pain and loves anyway.

So I will serve you a Deen's Doubles, a tasty nutritious vegan meal that my father created, and I will do it with pride and a smile on my face—no shame. Yes, I AM the Son of a Doublesman, and that's good enough for me!

* * *

"Memories are not perishable commodities,
they last a lifetime."
—Author unknown

Acknowledgments

Vitor Bill Hayibor, my Ghanian friend from Regina, Saskatchewan, who read an early version of the manuscript and was supportive of my first attempt to be a writer.

Reynold and Sylvia Francis, for reading the manuscript and for their detailed editorial input.

My wife, Grace, for her constructive comments and perceptive observations.

My children, Jeff and Alisha, for encouraging me to tell my story. Jeff was so fascinated by the details of the story that he funded our trip to Trinidad, in October, 2010, to retrace my footsteps, in an attempt to relive the memories. His editorial inputs were very insightful. Alisha's story editing of the manuscript was invaluable. She chose the title *Out of the Doubles Kitchen*.

My daughter-in-law, Padma, for her IT assistance in creating the website: *www.outofthedoubleskitchen.com*.

Christian Thomas, for his expertise that helped me stay abreast of the latest computer technology that made this book possible.

About the Author

Badru Deen lives in Florida with Grace, his wife of forty-five years. He graduated from the University of Manitoba, Canada with a BA in Economics and Sociology and a B.Comm. Hons. in Marketing and Business Administration. He followed a career path in Banking, Human Resource management, Marketing and Sales with the Royal Bank of Canada, Government of Saskatchewan, Philip Morris International and Nestlé respectively. Like his father, he eventually became an entrepreneur, running his own corporation.

Made in the USA
Charleston, SC
13 December 2013